SUCCESS
secrets to maximize
BUSINESS
in
CHINA

Larry T L Luah

Graphic Arts Center Publishing Company
Portland, Oregon

© 2001 Times Media Private Limited

This book is published by special
arrangement with Times Media Pte Ltd
A member of the Times Publishing Group
Times Centre, 1 New Industrial Road, Singapore 536196
International Standard Book Number 1-55868-594-4
Library of Congress Catalog Number 00-110099
Graphic Arts Center Publishing Company
P.O. Box 10306 • Portland Oregon 97296-0306 • (503)226-2402

All rights reserved. No part of this publication
may be reproduced, stored in a retrieval system,
or transmitted, in any form or by any means,
electronic, mechanical, photocopying, recording
or otherwise, without the prior permission
of the copyright owner.

Printed in Singapore

Contents

Acknowledgments

This book is dedicated to Amie and Jolene, my two beloved daughters, who have been most supportive of my book.

I would also like to express my gratitude and thanks to my dear friend, Leslie Lim, for providing me with the beautiful photographs in this book.

Larry T L Luah
2001

Introduction

China, with a population of 1.3 billion, is the world's largest country. Its double-digit growth (albeit the even larger inflation) over the last two decades has also made it the world's fastest growing economy. Its massive market, coupled with the strong economic growth since 1978, has attracted much interest and attention among businessmen and politicians worldwide.

To foreign business people, it is a place of enormous opportunities. What is behind the "bamboo curtain" has always been deemed to be mysterious and filled with uncertainty. For many, any attempt to do business in China is like "venturing into a minefield". This feeling of uncertainty is all the greater among westerners. It is understandable since the two are completely different in terms of culture and political systems. Contributing to the problem are many published articles on the "ugly Chinese" in the international mass media, which cause more misunderstanding and further aggravate such differences. While many of these articles are politically motivated, there are some which are by ill-informed experts.

For example, an article, "These Brains for Hire," in a popular periodical in mid-1995 described "Chinese scholars, who enjoyed wealth and power in their ivory towers, offering their services to the private enterprises". The writer was referring to an article in the local newspapers, which stated that government officials might be allowed to provide assistance and/or work part-time for the private enterprises.

Unfortunately, because of the author's lack of understanding of the situation, his article distorted the actual situation. He portrayed the Chinese scholars as well-fed and well-dressed government officials in big limousines offering help to the private enterprises. The truth was that these officials were not philanthropists but were doing so for financial reasons. In general, government officials are grossly underpaid and need additional income to supplement their meagre wages. In fact, the article in the local newspapers confirmed the authorities' acknowledgement of this situation and their efforts to provide an avenue for these Chinese scholars to get additional income. It was certainly not a situation in which the Chinese scholars had too much wealth and power and were doing so for charity. Chinese scholars might have the power but they do not enjoy wealth and their places of work are certainly not "ivory towers" by any standard.

Even in 1996, the official salary of a typical "Chinese scholar", for example a Director of Tourism in one of the provinces, would be about RMB850 (US$100) a month. This excludes many other perks and benefits which could add up to twice his salary. His Ministry or Department would normally provide him with a two-bedroom apartment, of about 50 sq m and a car, with chauffeur, for official use. A typical office would be a 15 sq m room which he has to share with one of his deputies, cheaply furnished with local products from the Government's Central Supplies Office. Ceiling fans are standard fixtures although air-conditioning units are becoming more common. In other words, the scholars might have some power, but they are certainly not well paid. Of course there are many that are rich, but such wealth did not come directly from their official appointments.

Well-dressed government officials who commute in chauffeur-driven limousines create a wrong impression on foreigners. Therefore, it is understandable that the writer of the article and many foreigners are misled into thinking that the "Chinese scholars" are wealthy, powerful government officials sitting in posh offices or "ivory towers".

Notwithstanding the negative impact of articles such as this, the sheer size of the Chinese market has attracted much interest and investment from all over the world. While investments from the US, Europe and Japan are given much more publicity; the fact remains that the main investors are the overseas Chinese who have the advantage of a similar culture with little or no language problems in China. In spite of these factors, there have been more failures than successes.

Like any other investment endeavours, successes are often exaggerated, whereas failures are seldom openly admitted. This is particularly true of the Chinese. The reasons are simple. Success is an ego booster and such publicity also increases one's creditability. Similarly, admitting failure means, "losing face" and more importantly, may cause one's bankers and business associates to lose confidence in one. Investors therefore seldom share their bad experiences with others, causing those after them to make the same mistakes.

Among the overseas Chinese operating in China, those from Hong Kong are more successful. Next are the Taiwanese. Most Singaporean investors fail to make the mark, despite the advantages of having a similar culture and language. A Chinese official suggested that it could be because they do not understand the business culture and are too concerned with rules and regulations.

> It is told that a Singaporean insisted on having a witness when he tried to bribe a government official in China. This was to avoid accusations of "pocketing the money" given to him by his superiors. While he was concerned about his accountability in the incident, the Chinese official involved probably thought that the Singaporean was trying to 'fix' him. Overseas Chinese from Hong Kong and Taiwan find this amusing.

In China, where the average official salary of senior government officers and state-owned organizations is only around US$200 a month, it is difficult to go "strictly by the book". Instead, it is important to understand the "wheeling and dealing, and entertaining to grease the wheels, environment" to get things done.

The famous Chinese war strategist Sun Tze said: "Know yourself, know your enemies; a hundred battles, a hundred victories" (*zi ji zi bi, bai zhan bai sheng*). In the case of doing business in China, the most important factor for success is an in-depth understanding of how the "system" works, i.e the mindset of the people and the business culture.

This book provides important guidance and information to the foreign business person who wants to succeed in China. Many true-life experiences are related to give you a better understanding of the mindset, attitude and expectations of the people that you will meet with in your business dealings with the country.

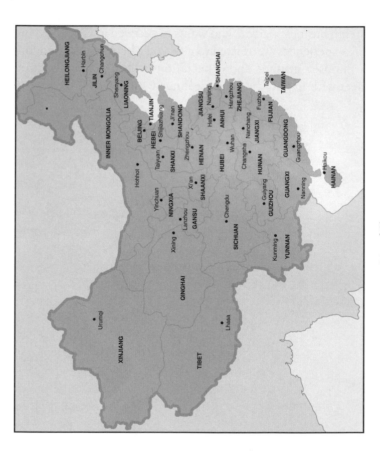

Map of China

CHAPTER 1

China's Economic Reform

Deng Xiaoping's Economic Reform Policy

When Deng Xiaoping was leader of the Communist Party, he was convinced that economic reform was necessary for the long-term growth of China. He prescribed a "socialist market economy with a Chinese character". The theory underlined the emphasis to restructure China's economy in line with the realities and problems faced by the country. It was an uphill task because there was no precedent or model available.

Open Door Policy

In December 1978, during the 11th Central Committee of the China Communist Party, a new program of economic reforms and an "open door policy" (dui wai kai fang) were adopted. A gradual and carefully sequenced reform program was emphasized. Priority was given to the transformation of the state-owned enterprises (SOEs), and developing industries and sectors that required minimum State investment and maximum utilization of local resource and labor.

The State, while still holding the assets of the state-owned enterprises, began releasing its stranglehold on these enterprises to the managers. In 1979, a Profit Retention Scheme (liren liucheng) was initiated. The scheme delegated decision-making to the enterprises and allowed them to keep part of their profits. The proportion of profits retained had to be negotiated with the supervising government agency and was fixed for a period of three years. This, however, led to much abuse.

In 1983, the Government introduced a series of taxes to guarantee more revenue and create fairer competition. This included a 55% income tax on the total profits of bigger enterprises— less for smaller units—and later an adjustment tax which varied for each SOE, instead of a uniform capital tax.

In 1987, a Contract Responsibility System was introduced, separating management from ownership. Essentially, the state-owned enterprise contracts to pay an agreed percentage of its profits to the State and take responsibility for its losses.

Agricultural farms were divided and leased to the farmers for a fixed share of their produce. The farmers were then given the right to keep whatever surplus they produced beyond the target or quotas set by the authorities. They were given full autonomy in the running of the farms. Farm prices were also raised, thus increasing the value of the farm produce. Farmers were allowed to sell their produce freely in the open market. These incentives resulted in a sharp increase in productivity and income of the farmers. There were also vast improvements in the quality and variety of their produce. All these were achieved with negligible State investment.

A state-owned supermarket

Productivity and yield increased but were restricted by the agricultural land available. Soon there were more people than land to farm. As a result, new entities called Village Enterprises or *xiangcun qiye* appeared. These enterprises were "collectives", owned and operated in a totally different way from state-owned enterprises. Excess labor made available by the population increase went into expanding the rural services and the manufacture of agricultural products. Such enterprises operated without State control and were run like private businesses.

The main reason for their success is the comparatively lower labor cost since wages in rural areas are much lower than in the cities. Furthermore, these Village Enterprises do not provide the kind of social welfare benefits such as housing, health care, retirement and other benefits expected of state-owned enterprises. Village Enterprises are in theory owned by the employees of a "collective" unit. Since they were handsomely rewarded for their labor, they began to produce more and better quality products than the state-owned enterprises. By 1992, they accounted for almost 30% of the country's total output and about 25% of the total exports.

Next, a massive plan to encourage foreign investment was put into action. Generous incentives were offered to attract foreign investments. Foreign investors trying to capitalize on the cheap labor and massive local market flooded in. Labor-intensive light and medium industries were encouraged to create employment for the people. Again, these were with minimum State investment and were similar to the industries that contributed to the economic take-off of Asian countries like Hong Kong, Taiwan and South Korea. The cheaper labor also encouraged many of these countries to move their production lines to China. Many products such as shoes, apparel and toys which once carried labels like "Made in South Korea", "Made in Taiwan" or "Made in Hong Kong", soon carried "Made in China" labels.

China's economic growth was based largely on domestic origin but foreign investments also played an important role, particularly in trade and capital investments. One must be careful when reading statistics on the massive foreign investments. For example, investments from Hong Kong account for more than two-thirds of the total foreign investments in China in the early 1990s.

Flaws in the System

While the economic growth in China has been impressive, there are many flaws in the system which hinder its progress. The economy is State-run and it responds to administrative decisions rather than supply and demand of the free market economy. As a Chinese economist put it: "the more centralized and more rigid the economy, the lazier the people; the lazier the people, the poorer they will be; the poorer they will be, the poorer they become and the greater is the need for centralization, forming a vicious circle".

Many of the problems encountered are carried over from the Communist Central Planning Policies. In such policies, industries produced according to quotas set by the Central Government. State planning determined the raw materials, energy required, consumers and even the end-users for the enterprises. Only those planned, got produced. The emphasis was on employment and satisfying social needs and not profit. Unfortunately, because of the poor data collection and communication system, what was planned and produced were often not what was required.

Until early 1991, under the Central Manpower Planning Policy, every state-owned enterprise was required to absorb a prerequisite number of workers from the youth that enter the labor market every year, irrespective of their actual requirements. This resulted in an over-employment situation, whereby one man's job may at times be handled by five to ten men.

As a communist country, Party ideology takes precedence over all matters even in the management of an enterprise. In all state-owned enterprises, the Communist Party via their Party Secretaries control the respective enterprises and not the Director or Manager of the entity. As the political appointee may not necessarily have the skill or know-how in running a business, this creates problems. Ideology and preservation of status quo therefore tend to triumph over business commonsense.

In 1979, Deng Xiaoping launched the idea of giving factory managers/directors full responsibility for the running of the enterprises. Unfortunately, the bureaucrats and party activitists, seeing their power diminished, were reluctant to implement this policy. Therefore, progress was rather slow. By the 1980s, the state-owned enterprises accounted for only about 50% of the GNP, down from almost 80% in post-1979. The report was that at least 40% of the state-owned enterprises were in the "red", but many locals argued that this figure should be at least 60%. It was even said that without the protection of an artificially low cost in raw materials, energy, etc, this figure would probably be closer to 80% or even 90%.

The unsatisfactory performance of these state-owned enterprises meant heavy debts, which they could not repay. The problem did not stop there. The bad debts among these enterprises meant that many of them, including the banks, were enmeshed in a "chain of debt" wherein a collapse of one enterprise triggered a chain reaction affecting one or many other enterprises. The Government could not afford to allow these state-owned enterprises to collapse for fear of the social unrest that would result from unemployment. Banks could not bankrupt these state-owned enterprises (SOEs) to recover the overdue loans; instead they were often forced by the State Government to pump in more money to "shore-up" the non-performing state-owned enterprises. As the problem grew bigger, in 1994 the Government adopted a policy to save only the larger state-owned enterprises and let the smaller non-performing state-owned enterprises collapse.

Problems Faced

Macro-Economic Policies

The rapid development of China brought many problems, which had to be resolved for sustained long-term growth. Overheating and the bumpy growth of the economy was caused partly by the lack of macro-economic policies to match the rapid economic growth. Essential instruments such as the law and tax systems were inadequate. The administrative organizations were ill-prepared and required massive restructuring. While efforts were made to modify the tax systems and law in line with the new requirements, they were not quick enough to meet the country's rapid economic growth. To complicate matters further, there were the people who were continually coming up with new ideas to "beat the system".

Infrastructure

China was practically isolated from the outside world until around the early 1980s. The people were poor and expectations were low. Right up to the late 1980s, most of the suburban roads were basically "mud tracks". Even today, horse carts, bullock carts and human carts are still a common sight in the suburbs of Beijing city. In many houses, a single fluorescent light or a 25-watt naked bulb is all that is needed in the living room. Water from the tap was considered a luxury as the suburbs still drew water from the wells.

Even in the major cities, infrastructure remains a major problem. Lack of infrastructure and utilities, particularly in energy and transportation, caused bottlenecks in many areas of growth. Right up to the late 1980s, even in big cities like Shanghai, work had to be done on shifts in some factories because of lack of power supply. Of course cities like Shanghai and Beijing have changed quite a bit from the late 1980s. Massive investments, both local and foreign, were pumped in to boost the infrastructures. Even then, more often than not, these were carried out on an "as required basis" rather than as part of a long-term master plan.

Foreign Relations

China's policy was clearly set on economic reform. It tried to minimize the impact of ideological differences on foreign policy. A lot of public relations work went into the exercise and disputes were tolerated to mute international conflicts as it focused on economic reform. However, China's success as a major exporter and source of cheap products also threatened some countries. Its biggest dispute is with the United States, which constantly threatens to impose economic sanctions on China. China's MFN (Most Favored Nation) status vis-a-vis the United States and its entry into the World Trade Organization have long been the subject of bitter argument and a strained relationship with the United States.

Current Economic Policy

China's economic growth averaged more than 11.5% from 1983 to 1988 before slowing down to about 5% in 1989. In 1991, the annualized real growth of the GNP rose to 7% and peaked at 13.4% in 1993. Despite its increasing dependence on export, the economic growth was strong from 1991 to 1993. However, inflation surged to 21% and trade deficit escalated. In mid-1993, the Central Government introduced tough measures to stabilize the situation with the objective of curbing credit expansion, reducing fiscal deficit and restoring Central control over expenditure by the Provinces.

The following measures were introduced:
- Curbing the growth of a rapid money supply situation
- Selling US dollars as an intervention to support the exchange rate
- Increasing the deposit and loan interest rates
- Curbing capital expenditure, in particular, the real estate sector

The Chinese Academy of Social Services and the State Statistical Bureau, in a report, justified the reasons for maintaining the Gross Domestic Product (GDP) growth at a relatively high level, stating that a sluggish economy would aggravate the difficulties faced by the state enterprises and cause a surge in unemployment. This report referred to China's first interest rate cut in about three years on 1 May 1996. This apparently was in response to pressure to sustain economic growth especially after the success achieved in lowering inflation in 1995. China's inflation rate was 14.7% in 1993. Its tight fiscal policy failed to dampen price escalation, which shot up to 21.7% in 1994. However, in 1995, it was successful in bringing it down to 14.8%.

There were different views regarding the relaxing of the tight monetary control. The State Statistical Bureau supported a cut in the interest rates, saying that the risk of fueling inflation was smaller than the risk of leaving resources unused. On the other hand, there were arguments that further slackening of the nation's tight monetary control policy would cause a return of the rampant inflation of the past. What was most interesting was that, underlying these statistics, there was a unanimous vote that growth had to be controlled at a sustainable level. This sustainable level is not even the 2% or 3% growth that many economies were trying to achieve. China's forecast for GDP growth for the year 2000 was 8% to 11%.

CHAPTER 2

Investment Potential in China

How Big is the Chinese Consumer Market?

China has a population of almost 1.3 billion. This figure includes the population of Hong Kong, Macau and Taiwan, as China has always regarded them as part of China. This makes it the largest country and also the largest market in terms of headcount. In terms of size, it is the third largest country after the Soviet Union and the United States. With one in five of the world's population residing in China, the consumer market is therefore enormous.

One Percent Wealth

An Indonesian friend once told me that, if five percent of the population in China consumed a packet of instant noodles in a month, and if he had just one percent of that market, he would be a very wealthy man. That illustrates the size of the market because 0.0005% of it would amount to 650,000 packets a month.

According to the 1993 World Bank Report, China's nominal Gross National Product (GNP) was only US$325 per capita, the lowest in the Asia Pacific Region. However, because of the social economic system where many basic necessities are heavily subsidized, the disposable income and purchasing power of the people are actually much higher. The GNP was therefore not an accurate yardstick. Subsequently, a revaluation by IMF based on purchasing power parity suggested the Gross Domestic Product (GDP) to be closer to US$1,450.

China's economic growth from 1979 to 1992 averaged around 9.5% and was double digit for four consecutive years from 1992 to 1995. In 1979, the GDP per capita was about RMB350. By 1995, it had risen to about RMB4,500. Notwithstanding the huge inflation, the enormous growth greatly boosted the living standards of the people. Such spectacular growth rate for a sustained period was only achieved by the Asian Newly Industrialized Economies (NIEs) of Hong Kong, Singapore, South Korea and Taiwan.

Apart from the phenomenal growth in GNP, China's economic growth was also apparent in other areas. In 1995, China produced 1.3 billion tonnes of coal (world No 1), 465 million tonnes of grain (world No 1), 95 million tonnes of steel (second only to Japan), 20 million color TVs, 9.3 million refrigerators and 1.5 million cars.

Its exports have also grown steadily at about 16% since 1979. Total exports in 1995 were about US$150 billion, making it the eleventh largest exporter in the world. Its imports were US$132 billion in 1995 and its market was considered to be less restrictive than that of Japan and South Korea. Foreign investment in 1995 was an encouraging figure of US$38 billion.

The Bund, the financial center of Shanghai in the thirties.

Based on a GDP growth of a modest 8%, it is estimated that by year 2020, China will have an economy as big as the United States. By then, it will also have an economy with per capita income of around US$4,000, or surpassing that of today's Malaysia.

The star performers in the development scene in China are Beijing, Shanghai and Guangzhou. Beijing has a land coverage of almost 140,000 sq km, of which less than 5% is urban area. It has a population of about 13 million. Since China opened its doors to the world, it has attracted over 10,000 foreign enterprises to establish offices there. Of these, more than 30% of the world's top 500 largest companies are involved. More than 100 international banks and financial institutions have started operation or representative offices in Beijing. Although insurance companies are still not permitted to sell policies in China, more than 100 companies have already established offices in the capital. Banks, insurance companies and foreign regional offices are normally established in Beijing because that is where the Central Government situates and where all the laws, rules and regulations are promulgated. Its 1998 GDP was in excess of US$24 billion.

Shanghai, with a land area of about 6,340 sq km, has a population of about 14.5 million. It has attracted almost 18,000 foreign enterprises to its central business districts as well as various economic development zones like the Pudong ETDZ, Minhang ETDZ, Hongqiao ETDZ and the Caohejing Hi-tech Park. The Pudong New Development Area with its land coverage of over 522 sq km, is the largest economic zone in China. This enormous economic zone is linked to the city center by superhighways via the Hanpu and the Yangpu bridges. Many investors prefer Shanghai to Beijing because it is said to have a shrewd and pragmatic government and business is dealt with faster. Its 1998 GDP was about US$44 billion.

Hongquio Economic Zone

Elevated highways in Shanghai

Guangzhou, the biggest of the three, has a land area of more than 178,000 sq km. Its population of about 72 million includes Shenzhen, Zhuhai and Shantou. It has attracted over US$100 billion in investment, or more than a third of the national total. Foreign funds were more than US$12 billion in 1998, mainly from Hong Kong. Foreign trade in 1997 and 1998 were about US$130 billion and nearly five times that of its closest rival, Shanghai. Because of its proximity to Hong Kong, over 70% of the investments were from Hong Kong. Investors from Hong Kong also account for more than 90% of all the export-processing factories. Guangzhou is known for its liberal policies which account for large smuggling activities and corruption cases. Its GDP for 1998 was about US$95 billion.

Does all these mean that there are 1.3 billion consumers for foreign goods in China? Though not quite this figure, estimates indicate that close to 500 million were able to purchase foreign goods at some point in their lives—certainly not a market to be neglected.

Who Buys?

A real estate developer once told me that he could not understand the "fanfare" about property development in China. According to his research, the market was small because only foreigners could afford to buy or lease the properties.

On the contrary, unbelievable as it may seem, most of the property in Guangzhou, Shanghai and Beijing are bought by the locals. This includes upmarket houses and apartments. This is an interesting point because, based on their official salaries, these local purchasers would not have enough money to pay the bank interest—let alone service their loans. Also, apparently, most of them pay cash and even when a bank loan is taken, the loan is relatively small.

They obviously have other sources of fairly sizable income.

High-end apartments

Is the High Growth Sustainable?

In the early 90s, many experts predicted that the economic balloon would burst because it was not possible for any economy to grow at double digit growth rate without getting overheated. Others argued that the pattern of China's economic growth with its matching high domestic investments and savings augured well for its future. Almost a decade has passed and the latter view has been proven right.

In 1995, China's 10.2% growth was matched by a 39.5% gross domestic investments and 42.2% gross domestic savings. A similar high level of savings and investments contributed to the high growth of the four NIEs. However, unlike the four NIEs, China's economic growth is not hindered by the constraints they had because of its enormous size and the relatively low platform of its economic springboard. It also has the advantage of a very large labor force and a huge domestic market. Its inefficiency means there is enormous room for improving the productivity and quality of products for export.

Many experts and investors have also written off the fears associated with investing in a communist country.

While numerous problems, including the overheated economy, exist, the medium term prospects for China's economy remain strong and promising. The implementation of the reform program has been correct and China is confident that its healthy economic growth should continue through the next two to three decades without too many problems.

Investment in China—Is it Worth the Risk?

Risk exists in business endeavors of any kind. As every business person knows, the rate of investment returns is proportionate to the amount of risks involved. A smart business person will minimize risks by acquiring relevant skills and experience.

Investing successfully in China calls for an in-depth knowledge and understanding of how the Chinese system works. Often, the "official way" is not necessarily the best way. To succeed in China, you will have to learn how best to get things done because you will find many a situation where it is better to be street-wise than academic.

Achieving the world's highest economic growth has meant that China is now recognized as a place of enormous economic opportunities for the next few decades. The 1979 "open door policy" led to the Chinese finding themselves missing out on many things which the outside world has to offer. They were hungry for almost all that they saw. In other words, opportunities for business are plentiful.

Opportunities and Incentives

The opening up of the Chinese economy to the world was probably the most important part of Deng Xiaoping's economic reform. The resultant high average growth rate achieved since 1978 changed the perception and boosted the confidence of foreign investors seeking to do business in China. In 1989, the austerity drive and the drastic actions taken by the government to curb runaway inflation and put the economy on track for faster economic reform also raised expectations for improved investment conditions.

The economic reform to attract foreign investments started with the establishment of the four Special Economic Zones (SEZs) in 1980: Shenzhen, Zhuhai, Shantou in Guangdong and Xiamen in Fujian. These southern coastal cities were former ports used by foreigners. This experimental scheme which Deng described as the "windows for technology, management, knowledge and foreign policy to better serve China's modernization program" was so successful that in 1988, Hainan Island joined the rank as the fifth and largest Special Economic Zone. Thereafter, several other Economic and Technological Development Zones (ETDZs) in the coastal cities, Coastal Open Economic Zones and High Technological Zones were established.

To attract investors, these special economic zones offered cheap land, ready-made and subsidized infrastructures, tax concessions, tax holidays as well as duty-free import of raw materials and capital goods. Government agencies were also set up to provide "one-stop services" to assist foreign investors in their setting up of companies.

The initial guidelines were to attract foreign capital, technology, knowledge and advanced management skills for the advancement of China's products and exports. Investments sought after were those in infrastructure development, primary industries, high technological industries, export-oriented products and those that could upgrade the existing industries.

Since early 1990s, these guidelines have been further expanded to cover substitute materials, high value-added products for export, transformation of state-owned enterprises as well as controlled development of the financial industries.

CHAPTER 3

Types of Investment Entities in China

Types of Foreign Investments or Foreign-owned Entities in China

There are basically seven types of entities that can be formed or invested in. The first four are the most common.

1 A Chinese-Foreign Equity Joint Venture

This is a limited liability company in compliance with Chinese laws. As the words infer, the venture is jointly invested, jointly managed and the parties share rights and liabilities proportionate with their respective capital contribution.

A foreign-owned enterprise in Caohejing

The investment can be in the form of cash or in the form of premises, land, property, equipment, material, technology or any other tangible assets. These other forms of capital contributions are to be valued in monetary form for determining the equity shares. Such valuations are subjected to the approval of the relevant local authority. This is the Government's form of control to ensure that the local officials do not "sell" the country's assets for personal gain.

Splitting of assets on termination of such joint venture agreements is clearly spelled out under Chinese laws and basically will be according to the share percentage. It must, however, be noted that all immovable assets remain with the Chinese party. Generally, the ratio of foreign investment shall not be less than 25% although the 1988 amendments to the Co-operative/Contractual Joint Venture Law waived this requirement.

2 Co-operative Joint Venture

This is a very flexible arrangement wherein the rights and liabilities of the shareholders need not necessarily be in proportion to the capital contribution. It can be an independent legal entity or it can also be a legal entity of any other business form wherein each party bears its own liability.

In most cases, the Chinese party's contribution will be in the form of land, land use rights, services, natural resources, labor, building premises, etc. The foreign investor's contribution is normally in the form of capital, advanced technology, equipment, management or even a right to, for example, an agency. There is no necessity to value the contribution of the individual partners involved.

Share of profits, rights and liabilities, etc. is determined by contractual agreement. Splitting of assets in such a venture is not defined under Chinese laws. It is therefore necessary to state this clearly in the joint venture agreement.

3 Wholly Foreign-owned Enterprise

This refers to 100% foreign-funded enterprises established by foreign companies, enterprises or individuals in China. This is a limited liability entity under Chinese laws. Generally, such an entity should be in the field of advanced technology or some other specialized fields and is subjected to supervision by the relevant authorities. Approval of such entities, for example, foreign banks and insurance companies, is limited and more restricted.

4 Representative Office

In China, representative offices can only perform activities such as data collection, establishing business contacts or connections, product introduction or marketing, technology exchange, etc. which do not generate direct income. A Chinese organization, which essentially acts as the guarantor of the Representative Office and is officially responsible for the foreign enterprise, must sponsor the formation of such an entity.

5 Compensation Trade

In such an arrangement, the foreign companies may provide the technology, equipment or other form of assets and are committed to buy back or export a certain percentage of the products manufactured by the venture. The cost for the technology, equipment, etc. may be paid back by installment. Such repayment shall be in the form of products produced by the venture or any other products as may be mutually agreed instead of cash.

6 Manufacturing or Assembling Arrangement

These are arrangements made between the foreign and local parties wherein the foreign party may supply the technology, equipment, materials, etc. for manufacturing and/or assembling by the Chinese party and buying back the finished product. The equipment supplied by the foreign party may be priced and paid back with the finished products.

7 Leasing

There are basically two main forms of leasing commonly used in China: financial leasing and operational leasing.

Financial leasing is where a leasing company purchases equipment chosen by the user and leases it to the user. Neither the lessor nor the lessee is allowed to suspend or terminate the contract during the duration of the lease. The lessor reserves the ownership of the equipment while the lessee owns the rights of use and shall also be responsible for the maintenance of the leased equipment. If the lessee fails or defaults in the payment according to the lease agreement, the lessor may repossess the equipment and dispose of it to recover the outstanding loan.

Operational leasing is the more common form of leasing in China. It simply means that the leasing company provides the user with the equipment required for an agreed fee. The lessor will be responsible for the maintenance of the equipment. It is also common for the lessor to provide an operator for the equipment.

Apart from these seven main categories, there are also various other types and combinations, for example, counter trades, processing or assembling, etc. An interesting and important point to note is that, under Chinese corporate laws, the individual has no legal standing other than as a representative of a duly constituted company or group of companies. Partnerships and sole proprietorships, which are common in other countries, are non-existent and not recognised in China.

Major Differences among the Types of Investment Entities

Equity Joint Venture	Co-operative Joint Venture	Wholly Foreign-Owned Enterprise
Status		
Corporate structure. Status of legal entity.	Partner structure. May have legal entity status. If requirements are met and stated in contract.	Corporate structure Status of legal entity.
Liability		
Limited liability to limit of the parties' capital.	Individual liability of parties to limit of the contract and/or the limit of the parties' capital.	Liability limited to the registered capital.
Capital contribution		
Specific minimum of 25% of registered capital for foreign party.	No restriction on capital contribution ratio.	Solely by foreign investor.
Foreigner: usually cash, equipment and technology Chinese: usually labor, land or premises. Set time for putting in contribution.	Foreigner: usually cash, equipment and technology Chinese: usually labor, land or premises.	

Management		
Board of Directors Regulated by articles of association. Joint management and operation.	If registered as a legal entity, Board of Directors must be established. If not legal entity, joint management committee to be set up.	Autonomy in operation
Restrictions		
Nil	Nil	Advanced technology Export oriented
Profit sharing		
According to capital ratio.	According to contract.	Only foreign investor.
Termination		
Normally 10 years to 50 years.	According to contract.	No perpetual succession.

Types of (Local) Companies in China

1 Private Enterprises

Under the communist system, the whole of China's economy was run and owned by state-owned enterprises and, until the late 1980s, private enterprises were hardly heard of. The small minority was confined to very small businesses called the *getihu* or private individual or enterprise.

In the early days, the *getihu* were run by private individuals who started their own business out of necessity. They were individuals guilty of a crime or an offense serious enough to have them removed from their company or *danwei*. In other words, their "iron rice bowl" (i.e. the security of their means of livelihood) was broken. During the early 1980s, the word *getihu* or private enterprise was associated with the term "bad hats". This stigma, and the fear of losing the security of their positions, prevented the general public from joining their ranks.

The *getihu* or private enterprises were confined to street hawking and handyman jobs. With the loss of their "iron rice bowl", they had to work extremely hard to fend for themselves. However, unlike in the state-owned enterprises, they reaped the rewards of their hard work. Soon it became apparent that most of those who left the state-owned enterprises were doing very well and earning more. Motivated by this, part-time private enterprises started to spring up. While hanging on to the security of their "iron rice bowls", these people operated on a part-time basis. Very often they would idle during normal working hours to conserve energy which they would put to use at their part-time jobs after their official working hours.

By the late 1980s, more private enterprises appeared. Some were doing so well that they began forming full-fledged companies. The stigma associated with a private enterprise began to change. While it still implied a "bad hat", now it also implied wealth. More took the bold step of stepping out of their "iron rice bowls", or what the Chinese called *xiahai*, "taking a plunge into the open sea".

2 *Village Enterprises*

Village enterprises or *xiangcun qiye* are small enterprises in manufacturing or services, initially set up to absorb the surplus labor. They have the autonomy to run like most private enterprises, and the authority to purchase raw materials and sell their products in the open market.

In 1976, there were only about one million of these *xiangcun qiye*. By 1991, the numbers were 18 million, employing almost 80 million workers and generating 25% of the national output and exports.

3 State Enterprises

State enterprises are owned and managed by the Government. Management is therefore totally dependent on State policies and directives. They are slowly being "privatized" so that while they are still owned by the Government, these enterprises will have the autonomy to run on their own. They are being distinguished from state-owned enterprises. Most Government administrative offices come under this classification.

4 State-owned Enterprises

Under the communist system, the State controls practically all industries through state-owned enterprises. Because state policies and a monopoly in their respective fields protect them, these enterprises are often grossly inefficient and badly managed. The State controls all pricing for raw materials, agricultural products and almost all essential items. These prices are artificially lowered to protect the earnings of these enterprises.

A large state-owned enterprise

State-owned enterprises are supervised by their respective Government organs, depending on the nature of operation, size and location. The supervising authority dictates practically every detail of the state-owned enterprises' operation; including what, how and when to produce, identifying suppliers and purchasers and even the pricing of products.

The managers are not given much authority except to carry out the directive set by the supervising authority. This is basically to produce the quantity at the time set by the authority. Profit and quality are not their priority or objective. Work performance is not tied to the "bonus" system which is just another form of Government subsidy for the low wages.

Targets or quotas set for quantity and budget by the supervising authorities act to discourage improvement in performance as any increase in quantity or reduction in expenditure inevitably meant an increase in quotas and reduction in budget allocation the following year.

More Hands than Needed

The communist government takes on the responsibility of allocating jobs for every able person in the country. This is, of course, a practically impossible task. With a work force of more than 600 million people, increasing at the rate of about 7 million every year, the Central Government has no choice but to simply send them to the various enterprises based on size rather than need. Each state-owned enterprise is then responsible for the welfare of its workers.

The result of this policy is that practically every state-owned enterprise is over-staffed, not by 100% but by many more times the number needed for the work. One young engineer in a bicycle manufacturing company once told me that, in his factory, only 25% of their current work force is actually needed. In other words, for every 100 workers, only 25 are needed.

These factors, together with the work attitude of doing the minimum possible, obsolete plant and equipment and the politically-driven pricing system account for the low productivity and heavy losses of most state-owned enterprises.

Economic Reform of State-owned Enterprises

To redress the situation, various schemes were implemented as part of the economic reform policies.

1 *Profit Retention Scheme*

Under this scheme, ownership is still retained by the State but the State no longer does the day-to-day operation and planning. The enterprise is given more authority in the operation and also gets to keep the balance of profits beyond that agreed with the supervising authority. This money, as dictated by the State, is to be used for production costs, bonuses, welfare, and development of new products and reserves. The principle for such distribution is set by the supervising authority but the enterprise decides the details.

This met with immediate success because most entities were barely making ends meet. Productivity and efficiency increased with the much needed incentive to performance. Unfortunately, the numbers that could benefit from this policy were small as many were loss-making enterprises.

Deficiencies in the system led to abuse. Since quotas and rates of retention were negotiated with the supervising authority, this created situations for abuse. Distribution of profit was disproportionate and there was even unauthorized distribution of such profit (records were falsified) for big bonuses and welfare projects such as housing, etc.

2 Tax for Profit Scheme

To control such abuse, a two-tier tax system was introduced. This included a 55% income tax on the total profits followed by an adjustment tax which varied according to the type of enterprise.

3 Sub-contracting System

Under this system, enterprises sub-contract the operation from the State, thus separating the owner (State) from the management (enterprises). They run the operation and guarantee the State a fixed return, either as a lump sum figure or a percentage of the profit as negotiated. The enterprises get to keep the balance of the profits and, in theory, take responsibility for any losses.

On the surface, this appears to be similar to international practice but there are many differences. While the enterprises have control over the management, pricing, purchase of raw materials and sales of products, including use of retained funds, they are restricted in many other issues. They have no authority over investment, import and export of goods and very little control over employment. In particular, they cannot fire any worker without the consent of the supervising authority. Their authority is also limited in issues on disposal of assets, business association or merger, personnel management, employment of workers including distribution of wages and bonuses.

The operation of these enterprises is subjected to the supervision and regular inspection and audit by the supervising authority, which maintains a very strong influence on these enterprises. The supervising authority also retains the right to appoint and/or remove the General Manager of the enterprise.

It also sets the target for the enterprise and is influential in determining its success. If an impossibly high target is set, the enterprise will fail no matter how hard it tries. On the other hand, a low target means a big margin for profits. While a target is normally set based on past records, it can also be arbitrarily set, depending on the relationship with the supervising authority.

For this reason, enterprises take care not to offend their supervising authority and therefore find it difficult to refuse interference from such authorities. Foreign investors with such partners should be prudent. Find out who the supervising authority is and ensure that a fairly good relationship is maintained. While new policies are progressively being adopted to improve the performance of the state-owned enterprises in particular and the economy in general, there are always new counter-policies created that reflect personal greed and selfish interest.

A recent article in a leading newspaper in China estimate that at least 40% of China's 100,000 state-owned enterprises are in the "red" and another 30% on the brink of losses. Many officials feel the figures are understated. Although these badly-managed state-owned enterprises drained some US$11 billion from the State Treasury in 1991 and remain a big burden to the country's economy today, rapid changes are unlikely because of vested interests and the social and political cost of putting all these factories and enterprises out of business.

CHAPTER 4

The Government

China, as a communist country, has had a one-party government since the founding of the People's Republic of China in 1949. In theory, the Government or the State Council runs the country, but in reality, it is the Chinese Communist Party that leads and makes all decisions in the Government as well as major State organizations.

There are three fairly distinct systems within the Chinese constitution: the Political, Administrative and Military systems (see Chart 1). The Chinese Constitution decrees that the National People's Congress (NPC), with its estimated 3,000-strong parliamentary members elected from the twenty-two provinces, three municipals and six autonomous regions (Chengdu became the sixth in October 1996) and the People's Liberation Army of China, is the highest organ of the country.

The National People's Congress nominates the Chairman of its Standing Committee. The Standing Committee meets every two months. It also has seven Special Committees which are responsible for drafting Bills for Congress. The National People's Congress also elects the President of the Republic, the Chairman of the Central Military Commission, the leaders of the State Council, heads of the Supreme Court and the Supreme Procuratorate.

The State Council is the highest organ responsible for State administration. It carries out its duties through the forty-one ministries, thirteen junior ministries and other administrative offices and institutions. A member of the State Council cannot be a member of the Standing Committee of the National People's Congress.

In the running of the country, all important decisions are taken by the Politburo of the Communist People's Party. The National People's Congress only meets once or twice a year and has very little power. The National People's Congress and the Standing Committee are responsible for the formalization of and amendments to the Constitution, enactment of decrees, rectification of treaties, interpretation of laws, approval of economic plans and state budgets, and appointment of ambassadors. It is also this organ of state power that appoints and removes (in consultation with the Politburo of the Central Committee) the country's Premier and Vice Premiers who collectively form the State Council.

The Standing Committee is the most powerful organ in the State and its members are all the most senior and powerful Chinese Communist Party members and Government officials. In 1999, members of the Standing Committee of the Politburo were:

Jiang Zemin	Secretary General of the CCP, President, Chairman of the Central Military Commission.
Li Peng	Chairman of the National People's Congress
Zhu Rongji	Prime Minister
Li Ruihuan	Chairman of the Chinese People's Political Consultative Conference
Hu Jingtao	Vice President, Secretary of the CCP, Vice Chairman of the Central Military Commission.
Wei Jianxing	Secretary of the Inspection Committee
Li Lanqing	

Chart 1: The Political Structure of the People's Republic of China
The three basic groupings are: the CPC System (the communist party organ), the government system (the administrative regime) and the military system.

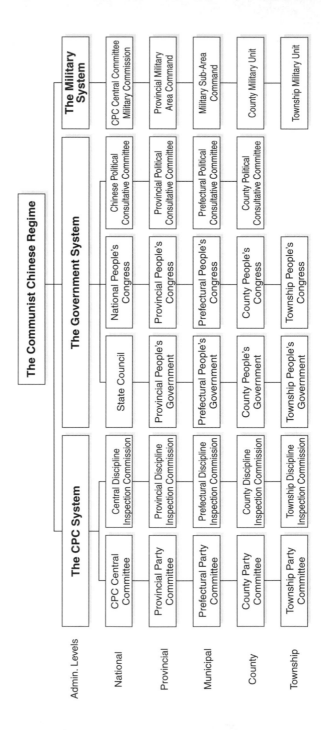

Admin. Levels	**The CPC System**		**The Government System**			**The Military System**
National	CPC Central Committee	Central Discipline Inspection Commission	State Council	National People's Congress	Chinese Political Consultative Committee	CPC Central Committee Military Commission
Provincial	Provincial Party Committee	Provincial Discipline Inspection Commission	Provincial People's Government	Provincial People's Congress	Provincial Political Consultative Committee	Provincial Military Area Command
Municipal	Prefectural Party Committee	Prefectural Discipline Inspection Commission	Prefectural People's Government	Prefectural People's Congress	Prefectural Political Consultative Committee	Military Sub-Area Command
County	County Party Committee	County Discipline Inspection Commission	County People's Government	County People's Congress	County Political Consultative Committee	County Military Unit
Township	Township Party Committee	Township Discipline Inspection Commission	Township People's Government	Township People's Congress		Township Military Unit

The Communist Chinese Regime

Chart 2: The Structure of Government of the People's Republic of China

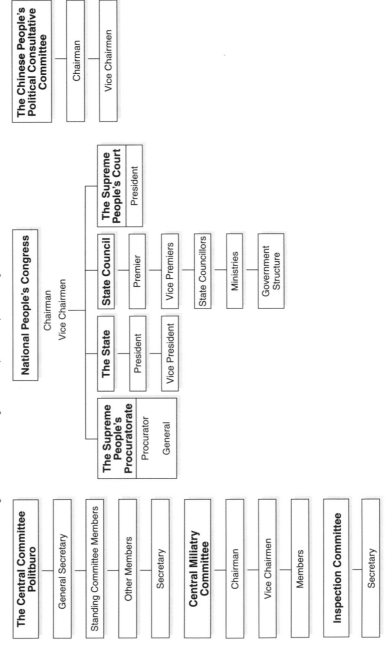

The Central Committee Politburo
- General Secretary
- Standing Committee Members
- Other Members
- Secretary

National People's Congress
Chairman
Vice Chairmen

The Chinese People's Political Consultative Committee
- Chairman
- Vice Chairmen

The Supreme People's Procuratorate
- Procurator General

The State
- President
- Vice President

State Council
- Premier
- Vice Premiers
- State Councillors
- Ministries
- Government Structure

The Supreme People's Court
- President

Central Miliatry Committee
- Chairman
- Vice Chairmen
- Members

Inspection Committee
- Secretary

The Hierarchy

China has five levels of hierarchy for administration. According to the *Statistical Yearbook of China, 1994*, in addition to the provinces, municipals and autonomous regions, China has 335 prefectures and cities, 2,166 counties and 48,179 townships. While the administrative power in the hierarchy of these five different levels lies in the hands of the Governor, whether he is a Mayor or Magistrate, the supreme power or No 1 in these administrations is still the Communist Party Secretaries.

Protocol is very important. Very often, foreigners make the mistake of paying greater attention to the Mayor than the Party Secretary. Such mistakes can cause more than just embarrassment. It can cause an investment to fail. It is therefore important that foreign investors and visitors take note of this protocol. Be aware that the ranks and designations used in China can sometimes be misleading. Take note that the political power of the Communist Party takes precedence over the administrative power in all Government organizations, state enterprises and state-owned enterprises—for example, the Party Secretary of the Construction Bureau is more senior in the hierarchy than the Director. Seek advise from the locals if you are unsure.

See Chart 4 for a structural outline of the Chinese Communist Party.

Chart 3: Hierarchy of the Chinese Government Administrations and State-owned Organizations

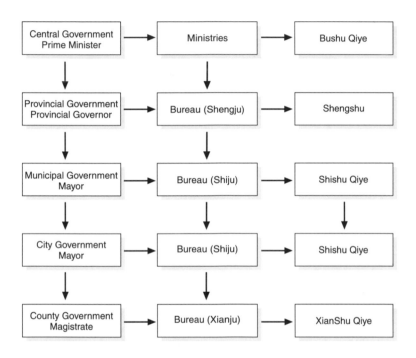

The first column shows the chief government administrator for each level of government in China. It is important to note that for each of these levels, there is always a Party Secretary whose political power overrides the rest. The administrative power may be in the hands of, for example, a Mayor, but the political "kingpin" is still the Party Secretary.

Chart 4: The Communist Party of China: Party Structure

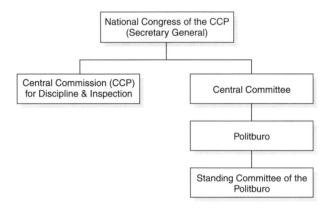

Ministry of Foreign Trade & Economic Co-operation (MOFTEC)

This is probably one of the most important Ministries that foreign investors have to deal with. It is responsible for foreign investment administration, laws, treaties and all matters regarding foreign trade and economic co-operation. Prior to 1993, it was known as the Ministry of Foreign Economic Relation & Trade or MOFERT. In both instances, they are better known as the *Jingmaobu*, which is short for the Ministry of Economic Co-operation and Trade in Chinese.

Before the "open door policy", all foreign trade was handled exclusively by the *Jingmaobu* through foreign trade corporations and other state-owned enterprises. During that period, foreign trade was governed by State policies rather than profit and other commercial considerations. In other words, trade was carried out to meet the Central Government's planning, quotas and other political requirements instead of profit.

CHAPTER 5

Land and Infrastructure

Land

Land in China belongs to the people and the State. In its pursuit of economic reform, China has separated the ownership of the land from the "land use or property rights". In other words, buying land in China simply means buying the "right to use" the land and not to own it.

Land in China is divided into three classes:

- First Class market—the State leases the "right to use the land" to state-owned companies or private organizations, including foreign investors.
- Second Class market—the party already holding the lease transfers it to another party, and
- Third Class market—the lease for the land is passed laterally from one lessee to another.

Motorola factory —a foreign investment in China

Land use rights can be conveyed by a grant, transfer, lease or pledge. Grants are only available in the first class market. It is issued solely to the State or its authorized agent for a specific purpose and period. Grants are awarded strictly on condition that the recipient invests, develops, and uses the land for a specific purpose in accordance with the instructions issued by the authorities and are normally the subject of a contract. The period of the grant depends on how it is classified for use. Generally, residential development is given 70 years; business and recreational and tourist-related development, 40 years, and 50 years if the land is used for industrial, scientific and technological, cultural and educational development.

The recipient of the grant may subsequently transfer or lease his "right of use" to the second and third class markets, provided he first fulfils the terms and conditions of the grant. For example, he must make the necessary investment or complete a predetermined percentage in the development of the said land before he transfers or leases the land.

Land use rights may be put in pledge as security for loans and other financial arrangements. In such arrangements, the creditor has the right to dispose of the land and has priority to the claim in the event of a default.

Like anywhere else in the world, land prices in China vary according to the supply-and-demand market situation. There is also the basic land value that one must consider in the purchase of any land.

Some of these major considerations are:
- Location
- Conditions of the land
- Availability of infrastructure
- Cost of development
- Prospects for development
- Lease tenure
- Loan conditions

Land in China is normally "sold" in its original condition or leveled and with the basic infrastructure. A land is said to be *san tong yi ping* when it is leveled and come complete with the three basic infrastructures or services.

Ping means that the land is flat or has been leveled. Check all claims. Make sure that the flat or leveled land is as you want it because a flat or leveled land can mean land that is 3 metres below road or flood level and you would need to backfill before it can be used.

Tong literally means "through", or the basic infrastructure being "connected through" to the said land. These are: water supply, electrical power, road, telecommunications, sewer connections, drainage, gas supply and steam supply. It is therefore important to verify what is provided and what is not.

More Than Enough?
Always bear in mind that your needs and expectations can be very different from those of your Chinese counterpart.

Examples:
- Water—low-pressure water supply and frequent stoppages are tolerated and even considered normal in some suburbs. Piped water is considered a luxury compared to water drawn from the rivers and wells or barrels brought in by horse or bullock carts.
- Electricity—expect a single fluorescent tube in the living room and a 25-watt naked bulb in the bathroom in most residences in the suburbs. Many roads in the suburbs are not lit. Therefore, do not be alarmed when the "more than enough" supply given to you is only a small fraction of your expectations.
- Roads—mud tracks are still common.

To avoid misunderstanding and unnecessary disputes, check that the services provided meet your requirements. Depending on the location of the said land, it can be quite costly to have services connected or infrastructure upgraded. Therefore, do not rush to sign a deal just because the land price offered to you is only half of what it costs two kilometers down the road. Make sure that you fully understand what is provided and what is not and whether those provisions satisfy your requirements.

A simpler way is to work out your own requirements and specifications and give them to your Chinese counterpart to provide the costing. If the overall feasibility study shows that the project is still viable, make it a condition in your agreement that your Chinese counterpart shall be fully responsible for the provision of these infrastructures for an agreed lump sum cost.

Investors, especially those involved in real estate development in China, should take note of the administration of Urban Real Property Laws promulgated in July 1994. These laws were created essentially to curb speculation in real estate in China. They cover the general principles on the use of land for real-estate development, the development itself, its transfer, leasing and mortgaging of property, titles and its legal liability. A developer is required to commence construction work on the land he has contracted within a year of the agreed date of the contract. If he fails to commence work within the stipulated one-year period without valid reasons, he is liable for a fine of 20% of the land cost or leasing fee. After two years, his land use right for the said land may be withdrawn.

The State Land Management Department via the Law Administration monitors all sales and transactions of land in China. Authority limits are set for each level of government in the sale and transaction of land. For example, at county level, the authority limit is only 3 *mu* (Chinese acres) for cultivated land and not exceeding 10 *mu* for other land. Any contracts that exceed these authority limits are automatically void in Chinese law. In such instances, the proceeds from the contract will be confiscated. Caveat emptor or let the buyer beware applies.

Infrastructure and Utilities

Before the opening of China , concrete or tarmac roads, electricity supply, piped water and other utilities were luxuries found only in the big cities. Roads at the fringe of Beijing were basically mud tracks in spite of its proximity to the capital city. Private telephones were rare. Most people had to rely on public telephones strategically located at the entrance to the respective neighborhood or village, managed by a few retirees.

With the opening up to the world, massive programs to upgrade all these infrastructures were launched. While the bulk of these were carried out with State finance, private enterprises were invited to develop these on a build, operate and transfer or BOT scheme.

The country is now well-served by an extensive network of expressways, roads and rails. Electricity supply, piped water, sewerage, telephone and other facilities can now be taken for granted in most areas except the really remote parts of China.

Subway system in Shanghai

Electricity Supply

Notwithstanding the expansion in capacity, the rising demand for electricity from the rapid economic expansion far outstrips the increased capacity. Power failure due to overloading is common. Except for the few main streets, generally the streets, sidewalks and parks are either dimly lit or not even lit. For normal usage, the electricity supply is in single phase, 220 volts @ 50 cycles. Electrical power switch sockets usually come with three-pronged "crow foot" outlets. Visitors with British Standard electrical appliances or accessories are advised to bring along suitable adaptors if they need to connect to the electrical supply. In international hotels and buildings developed by foreign enterprises, international standard fittings are available and are therefore not a problem.

Water Supply

Acute shortages of piped water occur in many cities, including Beijing and Shanghai. Because of this problem, well water is commonly used in certain areas. Installation of wells is, however, strictly controlled by the authorities because the indiscriminate drawing of water from wells causes settlement in the surrounding ground which can lead to the collapse of buildings and other structures. Rivers and lakes provide the bulk of the water supply. The water filtration systems used are generally old and ineffective. Quality control of the filtered water is poor. Because of this, domestic water filters are very popular. It is not safe to drink tap water.

Sewerage

This is a serious problem even in cities like Beijing and Shanghai. The population explosion caused by the influx of foreigners and the migration of labor has strained the system beyond capacity. Choking and overflowing are common. Because of this, very often the waste is discharged directly into rivers. Of course this is allowed subject to the examination and approval of the Ministry of Environment.

Telecommunications

The suburbs still depend on the public telephone system, but private telephones are now common in the big cities. Mobile phones are also very popular, especially among the younger generation. The only problem is that, in most cities, the lines are not enough and the old equipment cannot handle today's technology. It can be quite annoying trying to get through using your mobile phone. There is even a joke in Beijing about people looking for a telephone while holding a mobile phone in one hand, *na ge da ge da, dao chu zhao dian hua*.

The Oriental Pearl—Shanghai's telecommunication tower is also the third tallest building in the world.

E-mail and Internet

Many of the newer buildings boast that they are fully wired up with optic fibre cables for broadband Internet accesses. Be prudent and check that the main telecommunication network is not of inferior cables. Otherwise, it is like having a 150 mm diameter water pipe in your house when the city supply is only 25 mm in diameter. Having said this, it must be acknowledged that the rate at which China is expanding in this particular field is remarkable. Practically all the big companies like Motorola, Alcatel and AT&T are represented to capture a bigger share of the market. It was also reported that for the past few years, 70% of China's top one hundred new millionaires were from IT related businesses.

Postal Services

Postal services in China still rely heavily on the old-fashioned labor-intensive mode of operation. However, do not underestimate its efficiency. Within Beijing or Shanghai, you get your mail within 48 hours of delivery while cross-continent delivery may take about four or five days. Express mail and courier services are very efficient and are offered by the State-run postal services as well as international operators like DHL, FedEx and EMS.

CHAPTER 6

The People

Education, Skills and Attitude

Foreign enterprises in China select from the cream of its labor force by paying higher wages. In spite of this advantage, there is still an acute shortage of good skilled labor, the result of the Cultural Revolution in 1966 to 1976 when education practically came to a stop.

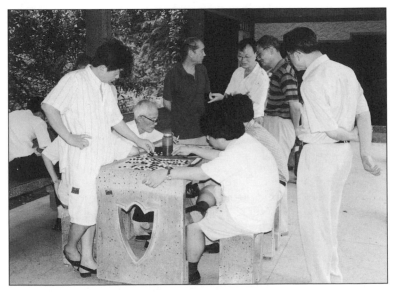

Chess—a favorite pastime

With the death of Chairman Mao Zedong and the end of the Cultural Revolution, schools and universities re-opened but the educational curriculum was heavily dosed with communist ideology.

No Work, No Mistakes

A young Chinese friend explained that "under the communist system, it is good to be highly skilled but such skills should best be kept private and not made known at one's place of work". That was in 1988. He then summarised the work attitude as follows:

- When you work for the Government or a state-owned company, you are but a small digit in a big organization. Everyone gets practically the same wage. The wage difference between the General Manager and the workers on the shopfloor is negligible although the General Manager gets better incentives and perks. So there is practically no incentive to push ahead. The general philosophy is to simply "float along" with the crowd.

- All these organizations are grossly over-staffed. The work in his own department of 30 can easily be managed by just a handful, meaning that it is six times overstaffed.

   He related how, as a new graduate full of enthusiasm, he had tried to prove his worth in his organization when he suddenly realized that he had everyone in his department (including his superior) turned against him. It was only much later that an elderly colleague advised him that he "should not complete ten items of work when everyone else in the organization is doing only one item". Obviously his action reflected very badly on all the others including his boss. The advice saved him a lot of misery. By adopting the same work attitude, he found that he had so much spare time that he was even able to complete his part-time study during office hours.

- Those who are highly skilled or think that they are highly skilled will be given all the work, especially the difficult tasks.

- The superior will claim credit for any good work done even if he had absolutely no part in it. But if a mistake is made, the subordinate will have to bear responsibility.

He quoted a local Chinese saying:

Da zuo da cuo, xiao zuo xiao cuo, bu zuo bu cuo

(The more you work, the greater your chances of making mistakes. The less you work, the less your chances of making mistakes. If you do not work, there will be no chance for you to make mistakes.)

This is the general work attitude of workers, especially in the Government and state-owned organizations. Although theoretically there is an incentive scheme, in practise, as can be seen from the wage structure, it is just another portion of the fixed wage. To avoid problems, a manager will normally make sure that every worker receives about the same bonus irrespective of work performance.

> **Mahjong and Guanxi**
> I recall an incident when four workers were caught playing mahjong in the factory premises during office hours, while another four watched. The manager who was with me admonished them but apparently, if I had not been with him, he would have walked past them. It was quite obvious that that was not the first time that they had been caught. From enquiries from the manager's assistant, I learnt that such incidents were quite common, not only in that factory but also in other state-owned enterprises. I was told that such culprits are normally fairly senior and/or have *guanxi* (good connections) at higher level. Therefore, most managers choose to ignore the situation.

It will take a long time to change the work attitude. Many foreign human resource officers prefer to employ fresh graduates instead of those with years of experience in Government or state-owned companies because of these problems.

Culture and Mentality

A great part of Chinese culture evolved around Buddhism and the teachings of Kung Fuzi, better-known as Confucius. Confucian is not so much a religion as a way of life and code of ethics, with its emphasis on obedience to and respect for elders, superiors and parents; duty to the family; loyalty to friends and sincerity and courtesy in all aspects of life.

This respect for elders and superiors, expected of all Chinese, makes it quite natural that an older person will receive more attention and be likely to be taken more seriously during a business discussion. Rank and status of a person also take precedence. Many foreign visitors who are aware of this cultural aspect carry special business cards with important-sounding titles /designations solely for use in China.

The business card is a very important means of introduction. As a foreigner, you will also have practically every Chinese you meet hand you a business card. The card helps you to differentiate between the many Li(s), Zhang(s) and Wang(s) in the various organizations or departments you visit.

Have plenty of business cards available during your business trip to China. Present your business card with both hands as a form of respect to the recipient. Similarly, receive business cards given to you with both hands. It is customary to study the card for a few seconds or minutes before putting it away. To immediately keep the card without even looking at it may convey disinterest or, worst still, disrespect.

Generally speaking, the Chinese are very shy people. They are polite, courteous and extremely hospitable to friends. However, unlike westerners, they tend to keep away from strangers. This may make them appear rude. They are often reluctant to start a conversation with strangers and are uncomfortable doing business with them. They prefer to be formally introduced and to have some references to the other party's background. It is therefore a good idea for foreign investors to get themselves introduced through intermediaries. Or to get to know their key personnel on a personal basis well enough before making a business proposition.

Incidentally, the word *tongzhi* or comrade used widely among the Chinese during and after the Cultural Revolution is a communist expression which means "same will or aspiration". Foreigners, including overseas Chinese, should not use it on the Chinese.

The Chinese consider their surname more important and it comes first and not last in their names. Address them by their surname together with formalities like Sir, Mr, Mrs, Ms etc. Addressing the other party by his or her position or title is preferred in China, for example, General Manager Wong or Director Wang. Expressions like *lao wang* meaning old Wang (for a senior person or someone older than you) and *xiao wang* meaning young Wang (for someone your junior) are common among old friends or when you know them more intimately.

Foreigners who speak Chinese should take note that some Chinese expressions have a totally different meaning in China. For example, *ai ren* means spouse or husband or wife in China and not lover or sweetheart as is used among overseas Chinese.

A lover or sweetheart in China is referred to as *nan/ nu peng you* meaning boyfriend or girlfriend.

Tai-chi and dancing in the park

Face or Mianzi

In Chinese culture, "having face" means to command respect and/ or have a high esteem or status among one's peers in society. Generally, the Chinese (including overseas Chinese) are extremely sensitive about this. An insult, contradiction or a sign of disrespect, especially in the presence of others, means "not giving face" to the other party. Making a person "lose face" or "not giving face" makes you an enemy for life. In a business encounter, it may result in your business failure even if you have the best business deal.

There are many ways to "give face" to a person: addressing a person as your mentor or chief/leader to show respect, addressing him as Director Wang when he may only be a Vice Director, and/ or going out of your way to accede to another's request out of respect, paying tribute to or praising someone in the presence of others, especially his superior or someone having influence over him, for good work done.

To reconsider a rejected proposal at the request of (say) the Mayor, is "giving face" to the Mayor. It is important to note that in dealing with Government officials at this or higher level, do not say "No" immediately, especially when there is a third party present. Even though you are certain that something is not possible, agree to reconsider or to investigate further. This need not necessarily mean accepting the rejected proposal. Having given him *mianzi* or face, you can then privately explain to him why the proposal is not acceptable. This will allow him to back off gracefully without hurting your relationship. Covering up an embarrassing incident, issue or mistake for a person is "saving face" for him. Such deeds often earn respect and loyalty and can be very useful when you need a favor in return.

Other occasions which Chinese consider a "loss of face":
- splitting the bill for a meal over the table and in public, or
- walking on the main shopping street with torn jeans and a dirty tee-shirt

The Chinese attach great concern and value to society's opinion and feel these actions show a lack of decorum.

Generally, the Chinese will not contradict any decision made by their superiors even when the decision is incorrect or irrelevant. Contradicting the superior, especially in public, is disrespectful and to be avoided. The Japanese have the same culture.

No, and the Chinese Way of Saying It

The Chinese are often reluctant to say 'No' to a request made by a guest. They consider this an act that will make their guest "lose face". They have however, various ways of rejecting or sidetracking requests. "To be discussed or considered later" is a phrase commonly used to delay the issue. "Inconvenient" is a more direct refusal. When foreigners become too persistent, "government regulations" and other excuses will be used to reject a request, but seldom a direct 'No'.

The One Child Policy and the Spoilt Brats

In 1949, when Mao Zedong declared the founding of the People's Republic of China, the total population was only about 540 million. With Mao's preaching that *ren duo hao ban shi*, which means that with more people, things can be accomplished more easily, a population explosion occurred. The population doubled by the year 1979.

To stop the population explosion encouraged by Chairman Mao, a drastic and very unpopular "one child policy" was implemented in 1979. Under this policy, every married couple can have only one child. This has now created a new problem: that of "spoilt brats" who will be the future work force that investors in China have to contend with.

CHAPTER 7

Labor

With a population of more than 1.3 billion, China has the largest labour force in the world but it is a largely unskilled labor force. The rapid economic development of the last two decades called for skilled labor. The Central Government thus started in early 1980 to rapidly expand the various institutions of learning and increase the number of vocational training programs. It was an uphill task because the people were wary of the Government after the Cultural Revolution. Many still preferred not to be trained.

Bicycles—the main means of transport

As more foreign investments started to flow into China, the Government began to realize the serious shortcomings of its labor force. In late 1980, the Central Government started a drive to actively persuade overseas Chinese to return to China by offering them various incentives and perks. However, the offer was not attractive enough by international standards, and response was only lukewarm.

Until late 1989, the Central Government's policies had discouraged rather than encouraged higher learning, for example:

Posting: Until late 1989, university graduates were assigned jobs by the relevant authorities under the Central Manpower Planning policy. Very often, the graduates were assigned to far-off places where their training and expertise were required. Non-graduates without any special skills were assigned to jobs within their hometown or city. This fear of being dislocated from home, family and friends was probably the biggest single deterrent to pursuing a university education then.

This policy of assigning jobs for university graduates still exists. However, because of the abundant opportunities in the open market, candidates can now opt out if the job allocated is not suitable or not to his or her liking. In fact, jobs in the Government and state-owned companies are no longer attractive or sought-after any more.

Wage Structure: In 1986, the basic pay per month varied from RMB40 for a new unskilled factory hand in the suburbs to about RMB150 for senior officials in the cities. Provincial governors were paid less than RMB500 (US$60) a month. (Now, apparently, the present wages are about five to six times more.)

Incentives for production workers such as factory and construction workers were 50% to 200% of the basic pay but were not given to vocations such as teaching and other "non-productive work".

Today, the increase in foreign investments has caused wages to spiral upwards, particularly in the main coastal cities and the

When the Butcher Earns More than the Surgeon

My driver, a bright young man in Shanghai, who could have won a place in one of the better universities, told me that he saw no reason why he should have a university education. The reasons he gave were simple and pragmatic.

- He did not want to be separated from his family or be relocated out of Shanghai.
- He could start earning money immediately instead of spending four years at university.
- Since he could start work four years earlier, he would have a headstart and have four years 'seniority over those who pursued a university education. Seniority in an organization is just as important as having a university education.
- With a university degree, he would probably be given an administrative job. Such a job may command a slightly higher basic pay but if it is a purely administrative job, he would have practically no incentives (depending on the job function) notwithstanding the fact that the responsibilities would be much more. This would mean a lower overall take-home pay, much less than that of a production worker.

He then pointed out to an old lady squatting by the sidewalk selling eggs boiled in tea leaves and soya sauce and said: *Gao yuen zi dan bu ru mai cha ye dan.* A rough translation would be, "the person doing research and development on atomic bombs is not even comparable to this lady selling eggs in tea leaves." (Bombs and eggs are pronounced the same in Chinese.)

This sentiment was repeated by the Deputy Director of a hospital. His basic pay of RMB138 a month was supplemented by an incentive allowance of only a few RMB. With a sigh he said, *na shou shu dao bu ru na zhu rou da,* which means "the person using the surgical knife (the surgeon) is not even comparable to the person holding the butcher's knife".

Special Economic Zones. As a result, strict controls are now imposed on labor movement. Foreign and Sino-foreign joint venture enterprises are required to submit manpower plans to the

Local Services Bureau which will then advice them on the method of recruitment.

An employment contract system was introduced in 1986 under which an employment contract had to comply with and be approved by the Labor Services Bureau. The employment contract had also to be signed with a trade union approved by the Labor Services Bureau. The Labor Services Bureau and service companies like the Foreign Enterprise Services Company or FESCO are government employment agencies, which in earlier days, supplied workers to all foreign enterprises. They still provide the employees with benefits and securities such as retirement, housing, education, health insurance, etc. which foreign employers may not be able to provide.

In providing these services, the employment agencies charge the enterprises an agency fee that includes the cost of providing workers' social welfare insurance and other benefits based on a formula set by the authorities. Gross deductions by the agencies are very high and can be even higher than the employee's wage. They range from 50% to 150% of the employee's take-home pay. These employees are technically employed by the agencies and therefore the foreign enterprises are somewhat restricted in implementing their own employment policies.

Because of complaints from foreign enterprises, the Ministry of Labor has relaxed some of the more rigid policies. Foreign and Sino-foreign enterprises may now hire workers from the open market and pay wages and other benefits directly to the employees. However, wholly foreign-owned enterprises and representative offices must still employ local staff through the Labor Services Bureau. The employment contract must be drawn in line with the guidelines set by the Labor Ministry. In some areas, approval of such an employment contract by the Labor Ministry is still necessary. It is also a requirement that the employment be registered with one of the few Government agencies such as

FESCO, where the employees' personal files (*dang an*) are kept.

For convenience, some employers choose to appoint agencies to provide their employees with the various benefits and securities.

Danwei

The word *danwei* was originally used for State or state-owned enterprises, but it is now commonly accepted to mean a person's place of work in China. There are many levels of *danwei*: state or ministry levels, provincial, city or county levels, and they determine one's position in the Chinese hierarchy. It is quite normal for the Chinese to enquire about each other's *danwei* at their first meeting. By doing so, they determine their comparative seniority based on their respective positions in their *danwei*. Once this is established, the one lower in the hierarchy will automatically adopt a junior stand in the discussions.

A leader of a *danwei* is more than just the boss of the enterprise. He practically controls the lives of all his subordinates. He determines the rank or position of the employees; their salary, job function, housing allocation and education for their children as well as the employees' ration coupon entitlement. In earlier days, he also acted as an agent for the authorities in the control of childbirth, overseas travels and so on. In other words, he is the master of one's destiny.

Like everything else in China, the ultimate leader of a *danwei* is the Party Secretary and not the General Manager or Director. However, since the implementation of Deng Xiaoping's economic reform policy, the administrative power in the *danwei* is slowly being transferred to the Director or Manager of the *danwei* while the Party Secretary retains his political power.

Income Disparity and Labor Migration

The economic progress in China over the last fifteen years, while rapid, has not been uniform. The Chinese *Government Statistics*

Yearbook 1999 gives the 1998 per capita annual net income for rural households as RMB2,162 and RMB5,425 for urban households. Coastal cities like Guangzhou, Fujian, Beijing and Shanghai enjoy the greatest gain while most of the inland cities were left behind in varying degrees of progress and development. The average wage in Beijing and Shanghai is five to six times higher (about RMB1,000 a month) than that in the inland cities. While a fairly experienced engineer in Shanghai earns RMB3,000 to RMB5,000 a month, RMB10,000 for the top executives is becoming common. It is useful to remember that the high wages in Shanghai should not be used as a yardstick. This disparity has caused unrest and movement of labor from the inland cities or even from the countryside to the major coastal cities.

Such migration was difficult and required a great deal of sacrifice from the migrants because, under the communist system, an individual's wage, social security benefits and livelihood are intricately linked to his commune and work unit. The Government keeps a record/file or *dang-an* of each and every Chinese citizen. This contains all the main events in his or her personal life history. The *dang-an* is started from the day of his or her birth and the main file is kept in the neighborhood police station. A supplementary file is kept by the school or university and subsequently transferred to his or her commune or work unit (*danwei*). Social security and other benefits are given and also closely monitored at the location where the personal file is kept. Migration means giving up the insurance, social securities, benefits and other privileges. So, a migrant from Wuhan to Shanghai will find great difficulty in getting a reasonably good school in Shanghai for his or her child because his residence and *dang-an* are not in Shanghai.

Local protectionist policies also make it extremely difficult for migrants to register residence in these coastal cities thus making the transfer of their *dang-an* almost impossible. Most migrants prefer to work for foreign enterprises where there is less significance attached to his or her commune and *dang-an*. Most local employees of foreign enterprises or Sino-foreign enterprises, which have minimal local involvement and do not have their own personnel department, will normally have their *dang-an* kept in the Labor Services Bureau.

Labor Laws

With the opening up of its economy to the outside world, China has set up a fairly comprehensive set of regulations and laws along those of Hong Kong. In general, foreign enterprises may, in accordance with their requirement, decide on their own management structure and personnel. The international practice of hiring and firing is allowed but within reasons. There are stringent regulations on working hours, holidays and protection of female and underaged workers. While the laws may differ slightly from province to province, the general principles should be observed and complied with.

Contractual Age

The legal age at which an employee may enter into a legal employment contract is 18 years and above. It is illegal to employ workers aged 16 years and below. Workers between the ages of 16 years and 18 years are also deemed underaged but they may be employed under these conditions:

- where there is no contract signed between the two parties, and
- where workers of this age group are not be involved in any hazardous work.

Female Workers

They should not be employed for extremely strenuous physical labor or any other work deemed unsuitable. During their menstrual periods, they should not be employed to work at high altitudes and extreme weather conditions.

Pregnant workers should not be employed for physically strenuous work or any other work deemed unsuitable for a pregnant worker. Female workers in an advanced stage of pregnancy should not be made to work extra hours or night shifts.

Probation Period
This varies and is determined by contract. It should not exceed a period of six months from the date of commencement.

Minimum Wage
A minimum wage system is imposed by the Labor Ministry to protect the people from being exploited. Such minimum wages are determined by the provincial, autonomous regional and other administrative governments and vary among the various provinces and cities. In the Yunnan province, the minimum wage for Kunming is 185 yuan per month, 160 yuan for Dongchuan and 135 yuan for the other cities.

Employers who default on this will be made to pay the difference plus 20% to 100% of the difference as compensation to the employee, depending on the circumstances. Another penalty of one to three times the compensation will also be imposed on the employer. The individual directly responsible for this non-compliance is also liable for a fine of between 200 yuan and 1,000 yuan.

Payment of Wage
Payment must be in cash. Time for payment shall be according to the agreed date. If the date falls on a public holiday or day of rest, payment will be made on the next working day. Payment may be made by weeks, days or hours of work, but if there is no agreed time, then it should be monthly.

Late Payment of Wage

In the event of late payment, the employer will be liable to pay a fine plus compensation to the employee. This varies from 20% to 100% plus another 3% to 5% of the outstanding wages respectively. The individual directly responsible for the late payment will also be fined an amount equal to 1% to 3% of the outstanding wages.

Deduction of Salary

The employer may deduct the following from the employee's wage every month— income tax, insurance, child maintenance, parent support, loss to employer caused by the employee, provided that the deduction does not exceed 20% of the employee's monthly wage and that the balance of the wage after deduction is not less than the minimum wage determined by the authority. A fine of one and a half to two times the employee's wage is payable by the employer if he is found guilty of indiscriminate deduction.

Overtime Pay

The formula for calculating overtime pay is:
    Overtime— 1.5 times
    Work on rest day— minimum double or once plus a replacement
    Public holiday—3 times

Sick Leave

This varies from three to twenty-four months upon presentation of a medical certificate. There is no difference between work related and non-work related illness or injury.

Maternity Leave

A total of 90 days is allowed, starting from fifteen days before the date of birth/labor. For those with complications or a difficult birth, an additional fifteen days is allowed. For multiple births, an additional fifteen days is allowed for each baby.

Retirement Age

For men it is 60 years and for women it is 55 years. Retirement age for women laborers is 50 years. They may opt for early retirement one to three years earlier.

Retrenchment of Staff

Retrenchment is strictly prohibited unless the company can prove that it is in severe difficulties such as a bankruptcy, a suspension of production, a lack of financial means to proceed, etc.

When the one-time retrenchment involves fewer than 50 persons or 10% of the total staff, consensus from the unions and workers is required and this shall be reported to the local authority. If the number exceeds 50 persons or more than 10% of the staff, the company may report directly to the Labor Department for its opinion and advice.

Calculation of compensation is based on the employee's average wage during the last 12 months and his length of service, using the following formula: Compensation = wage x years of service x 1.2 times month's wage x 0.01.

Termination

1   Employees whose employment cannot be terminated are:
    * Employees who are injured during the course of their work and/or suffering from occupational diseases.
    * Employees in convalescence.
    * Women during pregnancy, labor and maternity leave.
    * Other situations as determined by law.
2   Termination initiated by the employer with valid reasons and not requiring any given notice:
    * By mutual agreement.
    * Unsuitable during probation.
    * Severe breach of rules and regulations by the employee.
    * Dereliction of duties, embezzlement and similar action harmful to the company.

- Commitment of a crime.

3 Termination initiated by the employer with valid reasons but requiring 30 days' notice to the employee:
   - Illness or non-work related injury and inability to undertake any alternative positions.
   - Inability to undertake another position even after training.
   - Change in circumstances such that the contract cannot be fulfilled.
   - Bankruptcy.

4 Wrongful termination/breach of contract by the employer:
   - Deliberate non-continuity of the contract or delay in signing the contract.
   - Nullification of contract.
   - Violation of rules governing women and/or underaged workers.
   - Violation of the contract to terminate the workers.

5 Compensation by employer:
   - Loss of job—normal salary plus an additional 25% (of basic salary).
   - Loss of job security—amount of lost benefits and goods and services.
   - Loss of social insurance—amount of loss plus an additional 25%.
   - Conditions affecting the health of females and/or underaged workers—allowance for treatment plus an additional 25% allowance.

6 Compensation by employee:
   - Wrongful termination/breach of contract by the employees resulting in economic loss for the company and/or violation of confidentiality and/or secrets divulged to the current employer— all expenses incurred by the employer in recruiting new staff, expenses incurred in training staff (not more than actual cost) and cost of production, operations and business losses.

- Breach of contract by the employees entering into contract while still fulfilling another—an amount not less than 70% of loss of previous employer (borne by employee and current employer), all recruitment and training expenses and amount of loss incurred in operations, production and business.

Labor Disputes

In the event of a collective dispute, the company may form a committee to settle the dispute. Such a committee must comprise representation from the workers, the company and the union. The company cannot have more than one-third representation in the committee. A time restriction of 30 days is also imposed on the committee to settle the dispute, failing which it shall be deemed unsettled and application to the arbitration court may be necessary.

Breach of Labor Laws

Penalties and consequences

- Dangerous working environment—a fine of between 1,000 yuan and 5,000 yuan.
- Non-compliance with health and sanitation regulations—the company may not be able to continue work unless the requirement is complied with. A fine of between 30,000 yuan and 100,000 yuan may be imposed.
- Prevention and/or obstruction of inspection by the Labor Department—a fine of 1% of monthly sales and operations is payable.

Union

It is a requirement by the Central Government that every enterprise in China, whether state-owned, private or foreign-owned, or joint venture must have its own labor union. Union membership is voluntary and in practice, only about 50% of workers are union members. Many employees in small enterprises, both local and foreign-owned, and joint ventures, are not unionized.

Look Out for Hidden Costs

In early 1989, an acquaintance on his first visit to Shanghai to explore the possibility of investing in China, excitedly told me that the wage of a new waiter in a 4-star hotel in Shanghai was only about RMB300 (US$36) per month. I advised him to check further, because, to my knowledge, that did not sound correct.

Two days later and probably after further inquires, he told me that he found out that the figure quoted was only the basic pay. He realized that in China, the basic pay could be as little as only one third of a person's take-home pay.

Apart from the basic pay, most employers will have to consider:
• incentive bonuses, which can be as much as, if not more than, the basic pay and which are paid out every month as part of the monthly salary (Note: This is not part of the annual bonuses which are paid out at the end of the year), as well as,
• other benefits such as housing subsidies, health insurance, retirement fund, education, transport, food, clothing and even winter and summer allowances and so on. There are many more to be added to this list. Many of these are beyond comprehension. All these extras can add to a very large sum of money. For convenience, most foreign or foreign joint venture entities prefer to treat these as a lump sum figure.

Some general guidelines for the various allowances payable to employees by foreign investment enterprises published by the Beijing Government:

Medical expenses	7.5% of monthly income
Safety & welfare expenses	20% of monthly income
Pension reserve	20% of monthly income
Education expenses	1.5% of monthly income
Housing allowances	RMB30 per month
Commodity prices allowances	RMB30 per month

(This is exempted for State-approved export-oriented and high technological enterprises.)

Incentives	Varies
Insurance	Provided by employer

My friend discovered that the actual cost to the employer was eventually about twice what he had first thought was the wage payable.

In China, the Government or the Communist Party controls all the unions. While individual groups may form their own unions, they must be associated with the All China Federation of Trade Unions or ACFTU. The union leader is a very important post in the eyes of the Chinese authority. Therefore, almost all union leaders, whether in state-owned, private, foreign-owned or joint venture enterprises, are communist party cadres.

Working Hours and Holidays
Official working hours.
- 5-day week of 40 working hours.
- 8:00 a.m. to 5:30 p.m. from Monday to Friday.

In some cities, because of power shortages and other related problems, factories are made to rotate their working days to include Saturdays and Sundays.
- Lunch breaks vary from 1 hour to 3 hours:
  Foreign or Sino-Foreign Enterprises—normally 1 hour.
  State-owned enterprises—normally 1 1/2 to 3 hours

In some cities, an afternoon siesta is still practised. So do not be surprised to find beds in the local officials' office or, if you have a mid-afternoon appointment, find the local official /cadre rubbing sleep out of his eyes.
- Generally, Saturdays and Sundays are days off.

Official Holidays
- New Year's Day   1 January
- Labor Day   1 May
- National Day   1 October
- Chinese (Lunar) New Year—a three-day holiday based on the lunar calendar. Officially, the holiday is only three days but you will find that many offices are actually closed for at least a week. It is also prudent to expect construction workers and

employees whose families are in other provinces or regions to take at least two weeks off during this period.

Unofficial Holidays

Apart from the official national holidays, the Chinese also take time off for the following festive seasons:

- Chap Goh Meh · · · · · · · · the 15th day of the Lunar New Year
- Qing Ming Festival · · · · · · 30 February*
- International Women's Day · · 8 March
- Youth Day · · · · · · · · · · · · 4 May
- Dragon Boat Festival · · · · · 5 May*
- Founding of CCP · · · · · · · · 30 May*
- Children's Day · · · · · · · · · · 1 June
- Mooncake Festival · · · · · · · 15 August*
- Teachers' Day · · · · · · · · · · 10 September

* Dates based on the lunar calendar.

Wages

Labor in China is relatively cheap. However, look out for hidden costs.

CHAPTER 8

The Business Culture

An understanding of the business culture in China is essential for anyone who wants to succeed in business in China.

Guanxi

Guanxi simply means relationship or connection. In Asian societies, particularly in China, personal ties play a very important role in business dealings. It is Chinese culture to help another with whom one has good *guanxi*. A person is said to have good *guanxi* if he has a large pool of (normally influential) close friends, colleagues, old comrades and relatives, or the friends, colleagues and relatives of these people whom he can turn to for assistance when required.

La Guanxi to achieve one's objective generally refers to the Chinese culture of seeking assistance from relatives, friends and close associates. Often, these refer to issues that are not easily or even normally resolved if one goes through the normal channels. *Guanxi* gets you special treatment and consideration; negotiations are settled more easily, things get done much easier and faster, and problems can be resolved or even overlooked. It can be called upon for getting a job, a promotion, priority in housing allocation, getting one's child into a good school or for small issues like buying a branded bicycle. This process of seeking assistance is normally referred to as *zou hou men* or "going by the back door".

With true *guanxi* when a favor or assistance is given, there will be an obligation to the benefactor but returning the favor or payment of any kind is not expected. Among friends, when favors are given, it is normally expected that such favors be returned another day. This may not necessarily involve money.

In modern China, as the society becomes more materialistic, favors obtained through *guanxi* are normally paid back or returned in some material form. The culture has thus evolved into one that brings certain material gains. In many instances, *guanxi* can even be bought, as corruption becomes more widespread. The cost can be in the form of gifts, banquets, hard cash or even sponsorship for overseas trips.

Such avenues of assistance, or what foreigners refer to as "backdoor assistance" (*hou men*), is now essential in getting things done in China. To have good *guanxi* is therefore very important in both the social and business circles in China. Having more friends and *guanxi* means having more avenues to seek help or favors, thus boosting one's importance, status and value in the business world and in society.

Most Chinese now find it necessary to spread their network of *guanxi* as wide as possible and they take every opportunity to establish it as a social investment. To establish *guanxi*, the Chinese will send you gifts, souvenirs or invitations to a meal at the slightest excuse. You can also expect Chinese officials who have no direct connection to your business, to be present at your meetings and other functions. They are there to get to know the foreigners and people of high standing to advance their *guanxi*.

Corruption

With the open door policy in 1979, the Chinese saw the vast disparity in what they and the foreigners have. This quickly resulted in dissatisfaction and greed. In 1995, Transparency International, an anti-corruption organization, rated China as the second most corrupted country in the world after Indonesia.

Commonly-heard cases involve:
1 High-ranking officials who have great influence and authority. Queues of people seek their help.

Example: In real estate developments of a certain scale, the developers are required to pay a contribution that goes towards improving the city's infrastructure. The contributions required are stipulated under certain guidelines, and take into consideration the type of development, locality, the existing environment and so on. Such guidelines, like many other rules and regulations in China, are usually quite vague.

The classification of the development and the interpretation of its impact on the city's infrastructure lie in the hands of the director of each of the infrastructure's authorities. Depending on the type and size of the project, the classification can mean a payout of millions of dollars in contribution. Developers therefore try all ways to have their projects classified to pay the minimum contribution. These include "engaging" the officers-in-charge as consultants for their development. Apparently, paying these officers in the form of consultants' fees is permitted.

Example: An investor whose project depends heavily on receiving special incentives and other privileges will sponsor the siblings or relatives of the officer-in-charge for an overseas study course or even a job overseas. This is one way of ensuring that the investor continues to have the special privileges.

Example: When an enterprise has the budget for acquisition of accommodation and/or apartments for the staff, the local staff members will shower the officer-in-charge of the allocation with gifts and other goodies.

2 Officials who intentionally create problems so that they will be approached for help.

Example: I was involved in the construction of a hotel in Shanghai in 1986. Our local partner had a couple of very good people who did a marvellous job clearing much of the "red tape." The last stage was to submit applications with plans for the approval and endorsement of all the relevant authorities.

After dozens of meetings, lunches and dinners, we finally got the agreement of all the parties involved. However, there was a young junior engineer at all these meetings whom nobody paid any attention to because he was probably the most junior of those present. It was not until we sought the endorsement of approval from his department that we realized that he was the custodian of his department's rubber stamp.

He could not be found. He had felt slighted because nobody noticed his presence at the meetings. Finally, after dozens of visits to his office and numerous telephone calls, we were informed by his colleague that he was then on leave. His colleague also hinted to us that he had felt slighted and was trying to make things difficult for us.

Realizing the problem, we sought his superior's advice and assistance. It took us another two days, a few more visits to his home by our staff, his colleagues and even his superior, before he relented and finally endorsed our application.

We were surprised that his superior allowed his behavior but were told that he had very powerful *guanxi.*

3   Officials of state-owned enterprises who spend lavishly on themselves although most of these companies are in serious financial trouble.

4   Employees who moonlight at the expense of their companies.

Moonlighting Experiences
I had a personal experience with a group of construction workers who were idling on the job. In fact, some were actually sleeping. When I questioned the supervisor, he shook his head and told me that this is something foreigners can never understand.

"They are resting now," he said. "They may not be working, but they will still get their wages plus incentives and other benefits too."

"You should watch them after 5:00 p.m.," he added. "You can then see how hard they work when they walk across the street to work for the private interior contractor. These workers normally sub-contract the work or work on piecemeal basis and that is where they get big bucks."

A supervisor will not take adverse action against his subordinates for fear that they may have strong *guanxi*.

The job in the *danwei* may pay very little, but it provides security from cradle to grave. It is the main failure of the communist or "iron rice bowl" system.

A foreign business person employed a couple of salespeople in his Shanghai operations. As he could not spend his time fully in Shanghai, he left the day to day operations to the two employees. A few months later, he learnt that his two employees were also working for some other companies. On further investigation, he found that one of them actually had a full-time job with two other companies and was paid by all three companies, including his.

Reading between the Lines
On this subject of corruption, I would like to share some interesting "hints" I have heard over the years when your Chinese associates expect some "goodies" from you.

1 To *yan jiu* means to discuss, deliberate or explore.
   When it is mispronounced (intentionally), it literally means cigarettes and wine.

2 A request for you to *cheng shang ming biao* means to submit a name list. However, this innocent statement can also mean to "send in a branded watch" depending on the occasion and the tone in which such a request is made. It means a Rolex watch if "five matchsticks" is said.

3 *Jian ji xing shi* means "to act according to circumstances or situation". However, if "34 inches and color" is mentioned, then it means "action will be taken upon sight of a 34-inch color TV".

4 *ban shi yao kan qian hou* means "whatever you do, you must consider the past and the future". With a slight mispronunciation it can also mean "action will depend on the thickness (amount) of money received".

Corruption occurs at all levels in the hierarchy. This, coupled with the very complex networking system, prevents investigators from probing too far or too high up in the hierarchy. Often the investigators themselves, their relatives and close friends are involved. The result is that few are exposed and more often than not, a number of less important people will end up as the scapegoats.

Official Welcomes and Send-offs

On my first trip to Wuhan in 1993, I was met at the plane by a dozen of the local county's representatives led by the Magistrate himself. My entourage and I were whizzed off into the waiting cars without having to go through Customs. With police sirens blasting at top volume, we went through all the traffic lights non-stop to our destination. There was as much fuss in our sending off.

This is what the foreign investor can expect if he is invited to invest in a big project in China. The Chinese are known to accord important investors with VIP treatment and much fanfare on their arrival and departure. Be warned though—such warmth and VIP treatment can just as quickly cool off when your importance decreases.

Similarly, when you play host to a visiting Chinese delegation, it is important to receive and send them off at the airport as this makes them feel welcome and important. Your gesture will be appreciated and will certainly score you points with your guests.

Meetings

Typically, there will be many meetings when negotiating for a venture in China. Whatever the subject, the Chinese will normally want to know the people attending the meeting and also the subject of discussion. This is to enable them to make the necessary preparations.

For example, if the Chairman or President of your company is attending the meeting, their Chief, or at least his deputy, will be present. If only junior officers are involved, no senior official will be present, regardless of how important the subject of discussion is. Protocol is very important to the Chinese.

Another very important point to bear in mind is that, as a communist society, collective views still play an important role in decision-making. Knowing the subject of discussion allows them to make the necessary preparation. Depending on the agenda, you may find a large group of people, each representing a subject of discussion, in your meeting.

Punctuality is normally expected and the host will usually be in the reception lounge. The guests will be greeted at their cars on arrival and taken to the reception lounge by the assistants. The principal host need not meet the guests at their cars.

Entering a Meeting Room

The most senior or highest-ranking among the guests should enter the room first. The Chinese practice this protocol of entering the room according to the order of seniority. When members of the host organization escort you, this should not be a problem. Generally, they would assume that the first person to enter the room is the team leader.

Seating Arrangements

After the usual round of introductions and handshakes, the guests will be escorted to their seats in the reception lounge. The principal guest will be seated to the immediate right of the host at the end of the room facing the entrance. The other guests are shown to their seats in descending order of seniority. As this is the prelude to a formal meeting, a host member of the same order of ranking will be seated next to you to get to know you better.

Seating Arrangements in a Reception

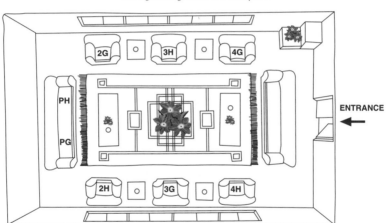

Tea and, sometimes, fruits will be served. After the formal introduction and exchange of business cards, a few minutes will normally be devoted to an exchange of greetings and small talk to break the ice before the meeting is moved to the actual meeting room. There is normally a large oval table in this meeting room, with chairs around the table and another row against the wall.

This is where the serious discussions will take place. The seating arrangement distinguishes the two different parties involved in the meeting. The principal guest will be seated in the center on one side of the table, directly facing the host. The others will be seated on the same side as their leader and in descending order, with the most junior farthest from their leader.

Seating Arrangements for a Formal Meeting

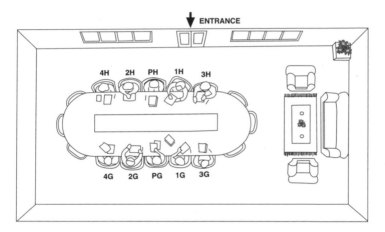

If it is your first meeting, there will normally be a welcome speech and the usual formalities before the meeting proper begins. You will also notice that every Chinese present will have a little notebook to record every word that is spoken during the meeting. Normally, only a few will speak during the meeting. As a rule, the Chinese adopt a passive role in meetings, preferring to take notes of what the other party proposes, with the occasional interjection to probe for more details.

During the first meeting, it is unlikely that you will get any affirmative answer from the Chinese except for what is obvious. Even at subsequent meetings, you are more likely to receive responses like *wen ti bu da* which literally means "problem not big or small problem." Many overseas Chinese and foreigners have taken this to mean "no problem" or "O.K." However, there are incidents when they were later told, "Look here, we told you there were problems, although not big, but you ignored us." Take note and do not write-off issues when the Chinese say that the "problem is not big". In most cases, you will need to do "something" to look into the "small problem."

Negotiations

Approach negotiations with an understanding of the mindset of your Chinese counterparts.

Expect negotiations in China to be long-drawn affairs. Such official meetings in smoke-filled boardrooms or meeting rooms can last for days without coming to a conclusion. It is the view of some experts on the Chinese that this is to show their higher authorities that they are striking a hard bargain in the interest of the company, state or country. Concluding a deal too easily means that they are not trying hard enough. It would also be a loss of "face" if they appear soft and compromise too easily.

The meetings provide a platform for the parties involved to get down to the nuts and bolts of the project and to size up and get to know each other, at least on the official front. Be alert to the various hints that are often dropped by the Chinese during these meetings. A smart move would be to try and find a way to talk to your counterpart in private. If necessary, go through a third party. It is the best way to find out the real reasons behind any problems faced.

It cannot be emphasized enough that you must remain diplomatic at all times and never ever "box" your Chinese counterpart into a corner, no matter how frustrated you may be with the progress of the negotiations. Doing so will cause embarrassment and "loss of face", especially when done in public.

If you are unable to arrange an opportunity to meet your counterpart in private when you first meet, do not worry because there will be many more. During the course of the negotiations, you will be treated to many lunches and dinners followed by karaoke sessions as well as other social activities. These allow you to socialize and get to know each other better as, generally, the Chinese do not like dealing with people they do not know or are uncomfortable with on a private basis.

Socialize and have fun. In a relaxed and private environment, the Chinese are more likely to open up and reveal their other considerations which were not brought up during your official meetings. Once you have established trust and confidence, the Chinese may even advise you on what is needed to clear the various obstacles to move on to the next stage of discussion. Personal relationship and trust is therefore paramount. Most deals in China are done over *ganbei* sessions, dinners, and in karaoke and bar lounges, and even in massage parlors.

Hosting Chinese Delegates

To most Chinese, the outside world is full of mystery and excitement. They have very few opportunities to travel abroad. Thus, foreign investors become their ticket to travel. In your business endeavors, you may be asked to host Chinese delegates on holiday or who are on a trip to promote China and explore business opportunities overseas.

You can be selective in hosting such visits but bear in mind the consequences should you decline. They may include people who can influence your business in China, whether directly or indirectly. How well you make their visit a great success has a bearing on your business. A badly organized trip or a reluctant attempt at hosting can ruin your business relationship.

It is important to understand the purpose of their visit, whom they want to meet (including your competitors) and the level of representation and hierarchy of the delegate. As soon as the trip is confirmed, a name list of the delegates will be given to the host to make arrangements for the trip. First, the host will have to issue a letter of invitation to members of the Chinese party so that they can apply for a visa and approval from their higher authorities. This is a good excuse for those without a passport to apply for one. The letter of invitation has to include details like the number of delegates, their full names, titles, company, positions, itineraries and purpose of visit.

A secretary is normally appointed from among the members of the delegation. The appointed secretary will be responsible for arrangements on the part of the Chinese party and for coordinating with the foreign party concerning the trip. You can consult him in the arrangements to make and plans for any welcoming ceremony (if high-ranking officials are involved), meetings and presentations, work groups, site visits, tours as well as entertainment programs that may be required. These should reflect the status of your visitors.

During their visit, the Chinese will have not only their business, but also their personal, needs to fulfil.

For the official part of the visit, they will appreciate it if you can provide them with copies of reports, catalogues and samples as they will have to submit a full report on their return.

On the personal side, sight-seeing and shopping activities are welcomed. As their trip would have been widely publicized among their family, colleagues, relatives and neighbors, they will have a long shopping list from these people. They are also expected to buy a small gift for everyone back home. It is a good idea to get a tour guide and interpreter to help them. Do not embarrass them by taking them to shops that are too pricey.

They also look forward to sight-seeing activities with plenty of photographs and souvenirs to take home as evidence of their experiences because the trip is probably one of the very few (if not the first) outside the Chinese territory. It is therefore important to arrange some time in their itinerary for them to do so.

Banquets and Entertaining

The Chinese are a very hospitable people. They love to entertain and be entertained. If you are important to them, they will find every opportunity to invite you to breakfast, lunch, dinner, and karaoke and massage sessions.

Dining is probably the most common way of entertaining guests in China. In most parts of China, because of transportation problems, many Chinese prefer to attend a dinner function right after work. Therefore, if you are hosting a dinner party and your invitation states 6:30 p.m., you may find them at the restaurant well before the appointed time, unless they have their own transport or are staying close by. It is therefore advisable to check with your local staff (or even your guests) a suitable time for such functions.

As a courteous gesture, the host should be at the restaurant early to receive the guests. In most of the VIP rooms in larger restaurants, there will be a reception area furnished with sofas next to the tables. Guests are received in this area and normally tea is served. After the usual exchange of formalities and small talk and when all the guests have arrived, the host will show the guests to their tables.

As a rule, the host is also expected to take care of all the guests' drivers. Normally the restaurant will arrange a separate table for the drivers. The food served to them is normally cheaper. It is also getting to be quite common for the drivers to be paid cash instead of being served their meal. Most restaurants in China will arrange this for the host and the expenses will be added to the bill.

Protocol for seating arrangements is quite rigidly adhered to by the Chinese. At a single table dinner function, the seats will be arranged as follows:

- The host sits in the center facing the entrance.
- The guest of honor will be seated on his right.
- The second guest of honor will be on his left.
- The co-host (belonging to the same organization) will be seated directly opposite the host.
- The third guest of honor will be on his right.
- The fourth guest of honor will be on his left.
- The other seating arrangements are less important.

When in doubt, check the table arrangements and look for signs. The table napkins, whether they are placed on the table or in the glasses, are folded in different shapes. The most complicated and tallest of these napkins will indicate the host's seat. The host will also have an additional plate on which there will be an extra set of chopsticks and a spoon. The co-host will have the same setting in front of him. This set of cutlery is used for the host and co-host to serve food to guests. If there is more than one table, there will be a representative from the host organization at each table to entertain the guests. They will take the host position at each table. Seating arrangements at these other tables are more flexible.

Apart from the normal setting of plates, bowls, spoons and chopsticks, you will find three glasses and a teacup in front of you. The glasses are for liquor. The smallest of the three (which is sometimes of porcelain instead of glass) is for Chinese spirits such as Maotai. The medium-sized glass is for wine, while the largest is for beer. If the guest prefers fruit juice or a soft drink instead of tea, a fourth glass will be given.

When everyone is seated, the principal host will propose a toast to welcome the guests. The small glass is normally used in this toast. If the host stands to make the toast, the guests should also stand. Eating begins only after the toast and when the principal host gestures the guests to do so. It is good manners for the principal guest to return the toast with a few words of thanks after a couple of dishes have been served.

During the course of the dinner, it is common for members of the Chinese party to start toasting every one of their guests with shouts of *yam seng* (drink heartily) or *ganbei* (bottoms up). The Chinese love to drink, especially with foreign friends, and appreciate a good drinker.

Dinner is over after dessert, and tea and a hot towel will be served. It is expected of the guest to thank the host for the wonderful evening, with expressions like, you are " filled to

Garden Hotel—a five-star international hotel

capacity". Very often your host may propose adjourning to a karaoke lounge or even a rubdown at a massage parlour.

In China, you are likely to be overwhelmed with invitations to lunch, dinner, karaoke and all sorts of entertainment sessions. It is important to reciprocate and show your appreciation but it is not necessary to outdo or even match every treat you receive. You may risk embarrassing your host. Gifts and expressions of appreciation are well received.

China practises a common receipt system. All local enterprises issue a receipt printed by the Chinese government which bears a controlled serial number. The local enterprises purchase them from the authorities and they are the only receipts recognized by the tax authority.

Unfortunately, because of the size of the country and its poor communication system, the government and tax department cannot keep track of the receipts issued, even though they are serialized. Counterfeit receipts that are as good as those printed by the authorities are freely available.

Beijing Hotel—a local hotel

The Practise of Inflating Bills

One interesting experience I had was during my first few trips to China in the mid-1980s. Our host attended to us from the hour we landed: at breakfast, lunch, dinner and karaoke, he paid every single bill. After three days and embarrassed by all the hospitality and generosity, I tried to reciprocate by rushing for the bill after an expensive dinner. My local staff, ZhangYong, quickly held me back and whispered that he would explain later. Rather upset by his action, I sat back and allowed our host to proceed to the counter to pay the bill.

The next day, ZhangYong suggested that I take all the local staff to dinner. When dinner was over, as I tried to get the attention of the waitress for the bill, ZhangYong again held me back and instead asked me to pay at the counter. Puzzled, I went to the cashier's counter to ask for the bill. The total bill was about RMB1,000. I paid the amount plus a tip. The cashier then surprised me by asking, "How much do you want on the receipt?" I thought I had heard her wrong. She repeated the question. I told her to write the amount I had paid. She looked at me in disbelief but handed me the receipt for RMB1,000.

Back at the table, ZhangYong and my local staff were all smiles when I walked towards them. I told him what had happened and he laughed. He then explained that it is an unwritten rule in some of these restaurants to make out an inflated receipt when you pay at the counter. (This does not happen when you pay at your table). So, if your bill is RMB1,000, the restaurant can write you a receipt for say, RMB1,500. This allows the patrons to claim more from their company. To the restaurant operators, it is an incentive to attract customers. Also, patrons will never complain if they are overcharged.

The falsified receipts are not recorded in their accounts. It is quite common for the restaurants to have more than one set of accounts and so avoid paying the additional taxes.

Night Life in China

Prostitution, nightclubs/cabarets, discos, karaokes, massage parlors and pubs flourished with the influx of foreigners. There were more of such establishments in the big cities of Shanghai, Guangzhou and Chengdu than any other cities in Asia.

There are two types of karaoke lounges—one, where you can sing among yourselves, and the other which provides a hostess to serve you and keep you company while you sing. Places with hostesses can be extremely expensive. So if you plan a night out in such places, do check out the charges first.

Also available in most parts of China are many types and styles of massage. Most of the masseur/masseuse are Chinese physicians specializing in various forms of therapy. There are also the visually handicapped who are specially trained to provide such therapy. Last but not least, there are also massage parlors that provide young attractive ladies. Many massage parlors are very well equipped with saunas, steam baths and mini theater lounges. Some even provide hair grooming facilities as well as manicure and pedicure.

Tipping

Under the Communist ruling, tipping is considered unacceptable and associated with bourgeois practices. Of course this is no longer applicable now. But you can still find some Chinese, especially older ones, in smaller towns and cities refusing tips offered to them. In the bigger cities, tipping is appropriate and often expected.

Gifts and Souvenirs

It is customary for the Chinese to present foreign guests, visitors and business associates with small gifts or souvenirs. These will normally be a local product like cloisonné ware, porcelain, lacquer, pottery, paper-cuts, Chinese painting or calligraphy.

It is necessary to return the goodwill gesture. Gifts or souvenirs should be commensurate with the importance and position of the other party, your business or other endeavors and the circumstances involved. Items like a clock or a green hat are taboo as clocks are associated with death and green hats with cuckolds.

In general, the Chinese expect the gifts they receive from foreigners to be of greater value. Gifts and souvenirs given by the local enterprises are normally purchased with State funds but the gifts and souvenirs they receive are kept for their own use. This has encouraged abuse in the use of Government funds. Officials present gifts and souvenirs indiscriminately in the hope of having their gesture reciprocated.

The Importance of Drivers

Unlike in most other countries, drivers in China are quite well paid compared to the other professions. Driving is therefore a much sought-after profession and has a fairly high status in their society.

Drivers in the Government service or state-owned enterprises have a very close relationship with their bosses and are with them most of the time. Do not be alarmed to find them behaving like 'buddies' dining at the same table as their bosses. You may also find them at the karaoke bars singing along with the bosses and, at times, even in the meeting room when negotiation is in progress.

Driving was a prestigious job especially in the mid-1980s. At that time, there were very few cars and one actually needed to have *guanxi* or "back door assistance" to be selected for a driving class. Bosses with drivers are at the top echelons of their society and the drivers also act as their bodyguards. In the early days, drivers were mostly ex-military personnel often trained in combat and anti-espionage.

Government officials in China do not normally have a secretary. Instead, they have a personal assistant, and very often you find the driver doubling up as the personal assistant. So never underestimate the influence drivers have. They can make very useful allies. It is therefore understandable that the Chinese consider driving a prestigious job.

More than Driving

My personal experience with drivers was in Shanghai in the mid 1980s. Our local partner recommended a driver to me. He was an ex-army officer working as a taxi driver in one of the state - owned taxi companies. He was young, intelligent, very unassuming and we got along pretty well. It was only after about a year that he admitted to me in private that he had actually kept a fairly detailed record of my activities in Shanghai and these were submitted to his work unit on a regular basis. He also explained that it was a normal practice in China then. When I met him again in the nineties, he told me that the practice had been discontinued. Nevertheless, if you are in a remote part of China, it is prudent to be cautious.

CHAPTER 9

General Business Information

Foreign Exchange Control

When China had a closed economy, foreign exchange control was never an issue. However, with the opening up of its market to the world, this became an important issue. In 1978, at the eleventh National People's Congress, the need for foreign exchange legislation was addressed. In 1980, the State Council promulgated the first legislation on foreign exchange. A State Administration of Exchange Control under the People's Bank of China was established to implement and control all matters on foreign exchange.

At first, foreigners in China were prohibited from using the local currency, or renminbi. A Foreign Exchange Certificate (FEC) in place of the renminbi was introduced exclusively for use by foreigners in China. However, because the FEC could be freely converted to US$ and other foreign currencies, it developed a black market value which at one stage was almost twice the value of the renminbi.

As the renminbi was not convertible, foreign investors faced serious problems in foreign imports and in repatriating their earnings and balancing their foreign exchange cash flow. Faced with mounting pressure from investors, Foreign Exchange Centers or "swap centers" were established in all major cities in China. At these centers, foreign investors and Chinese enterprises could swap their currencies at the predetermined rates set by the government. The rates used were normally much lower than the black-market rates and buyers for the renminbi were limited. Nevertheless, it was a big step forward and a relief to foreign investors.

The enormous success of the economic development and the great demand for foreign exchange soon proved the system ineffective. To maintain and enhance a healthy development of its economy through the "open door policy", China had to move towards a system which allowed its currency to be converted more freely. Various reforms and changes were made to the foreign exchange policy, with then Vice Premier Zhu Rongji assuring the world that the renminbi would eventually be made freely convertible.

Measures introduced were:
- unifying the variable market rates for renminbi at swap centers (or Foreign Exchange Adjustment Centers) throughout China
- establishing official exchange rates based on national market averages in the swap centers and the China Foreign Exchange Trading System (CFETS)
- removing the Foreign Exchange Certificate (FEC) for a unified currency
- creating the China Foreign Exchange Trading System to replace the swap centers
- creating regional inter-bank swap markets under CFETS inter-bank market
- introducing over-the-counter trading at commercial banks

Restructuring the Banking System

With the new economy, China had to restructure its banking system in line with the new market economy and international banking practices. In the restructuring, the rigid state control was abandoned.

The People's Bank of China was transformed into a commercial bank and also acted as China's central bank. Its roles included the planning, implementation and control of all monetary policies, issue of currency and regulating the volume and scale of loans and interest rates as well as exercising strict control over all the banking institutions in China.

Foreign banking and other financial services were allowed entry into the Chinese market under the various stages of liberalization. State-owned banks remained the mainstay while co-existing with foreign and other financial institutions.

Loans and Financing for Foreign Investments

Foreign investors are allowed to take loans from the Bank of China or other domestic banks or financial institutions approved by the Bank of China. They may also borrow in foreign exchange directly from a foreign or foreign-funded bank or other financial institutions, as long as these transactions are registered with the State Administration of Exchange Control.

There are two main types of loans available. The first and bigger loan is for investments in fixed assets—construction, purchase and/or installation of major equipment or machinery. It can be in the form of a project loan or a short- or medium-term loan. The second type is for working capital such as production and operational financing. It is normally in the form of a production or operational loan, overdraft or other short-term loans.

Pudong Lujiazui financial center

Conditions for loans

The Bank of China exercises strict control on loans. Some of the general conditions are:

- The investor has a valid business license
- The investor has an account with the Bank of China
- The registered capital of the business has been duly paid as stipulated by the laws.
- The loan has been confirmed and authorized by the Board of Directors.
- The business must prove that it is capable of repaying the loan.
- An approved guarantor for the repayment of loan plus interest is required.
- If the loan is in foreign exchange from a foreign-funded institution, the loan must be accompanied by a guarantee in foreign exchange settlement. In the event of a default, the guarantor must discharge its obligation in foreign exchange.

Letter of Credit

Two very important points regarding the Letter of Credit in China should be noted:

- China is not a member of the International Chamber Of Commerce (ICC) and is therefore not under any obligation to conform to the International Chamber of Commerce's uniform Customs and Practises for documentary credits, although in practise it does comply with all the rules.
- Letters of Credit issued by China are usually not a confirmation. They merely advice and all transactions must be cleared through the Bank of China.

Foreign Trade

Exports

Exports of essential goods are controlled by the State via central licenses and quotas. This practise raised objections from China's trading partners. In its efforts to gain admission into GATT and the WTO, China began relaxing its tight control over various items and practises. In 1991, all State subsidies for export were abolished, and central licensing and quota control for many of the goods were removed.

Exports of important minerals like copper, plutonium and its alloys are banned. Some of the other minerals, natural resources and produce are directly controlled by the State. These include crude oil, coal, rice, and soya beans. Apart from these, the Chinese foreign trade enterprises have no trade restrictions except those imposed by bilateral trade agreements.

Foreign-funded enterprises can, and are encouraged to, export their products. Those dealing with products for local consumption are encouraged to buy local raw materials and other products with the local currency they earn, and export them for foreign exchange.

Imports

China has always been very careful with its control over imports. Fear of trade imbalance and import of "undesirable" products as well as protection of its local industries require that it exercises strict control. In its efforts to join GATT and the WTO, China has cut its import subsidies on certain products, mainly agricultural, and reduced taxes on imports to the level approved by GATT. The number of items requiring import license has been reduced and processing of such licenses speeded up.

Documents

The Chinese normally stamp all documents—including cheques, invoices, bills of lading, and insurance certificates—with a company stamp instead of sign them. Notarization of these documents is, however, readily available in all major cities in China.

All contracts and important documents will have to be in Chinese. You may have a translated version in English or another language, but the Chinese version of these documents takes precedence.

Customs

Two state-owned organizations, the China National Foreign Trade Transportation Corporation and the China Ocean Shipping Agency, handle all cargo imported or exported by air, sea or land through the Chinese ports. They act as authorizing agents for port clearance and delivery of the goods in transit through the Chinese ports. They also provide services like insurance and making of claims where necessary. The Customs facilities are under the control of the General Administration of Customs which is directly under the State Council.

Copyright and Intellectual Property

Everything in the country belongs to the State. Disputes on copyright and intellectual property are therefore only between state-owned organizations and are easily resolved by the higher authorities. With the introduction of the economic reform policy and the influx of foreign trade and investment, copyright issues have become an urgent matter to be resolved.

The trademark law came into effect in 1982 and a trademark registration agency under the China Council for the Promotion of International Trade or CCPIT was established in Beijing. China joined the Paris Convention in 1985 which allowed individuals and enterprises to register patents on inventions, designs and enjoy protection from infringement. As part of its efforts to join GATT and the WTO, China established copyright laws in 1991 and became a signatory to the Berne Copyright Convention and the Universal Copyright Convention in 1992.

The Chinese Government's efforts to assure the rest of the world that it respects their rights is a comfort to its trading partners and foreign investors. However, notwithstanding the Government's efforts, foreign companies should register their patents and copyrights with the Chinese authorities as soon as possible and use lawyers specializing in Chinese commercial law for the purpose.

Land Ownership

Can a foreign business person own land in China? What are the laws governing the ownership, lease and transfer of land and what is the difference between "owning the lease of a piece of land" and "having the rights of use for a piece of land"?

China separates "land ownership" from "land use rights". Generally, all land is controlled and administered by the State Land Bureau. At the municipal and provincial levels, they are controlled by the municipal or provincial land administration bureau which assigns the land to the city, county and district land offices which, in turn, assign the "rights of use" to the various local organizations and individual. The law allows the transfer of lease only. When you "buy a piece of land", you are actually buying the "lease for the land use rights" and not the ownership of the land.

Since the local organizations and individuals also belong to the country, such "rights of use" normally do not have a period of validity. If your local business partner(s) says that the land is "freehold," it simply means that the government has assigned it to him. If a request is made for the transfer of such "rights of use" to a Sino-foreign joint venture, a lease period for the land will be given.

Land use rights are conveyed by means of a grant, a transfer, a lease, or a pledge. Grants are only for the first class market. They are for a specific period and are conveyed solely by the State or its authorized agent in exchange for payment of the full assignment fees in advance. A grant is normally quite restrictive and the recipient is required to invest, develop and/or use the land for a specific purpose according to the conditions of the contract stipulated by the local planning, construction and real estate department.

Acquisition of "rights of use through assignment or grant" or *hua po tu di* is much cheaper because of the lower costs for land, contributions to infrastructures, utilities and even taxes. The biggest disadvantage is that you do not "own the land." If you build a factory, apartments or a commercial complex on this land, you have to either use it or lease it. You cannot sell or transfer them to a third party.

Acquisition of land by "outright lease/transfer" or *pi zu* basically applies to foreign and Sino-foreign joint ventures. This outright purchase of the lease of the land is for a fixed period. State legislation restricts the lease period as follows:

residential use	70 years
commercial use	50 years
industrial use	50 years
tourism	40 years
others	50 years

In such a transaction, a "land title" or *hong ben* (a certificate bound in red), will be issued as proof of ownership of the lease. You may sell, transfer or mortgage such land and/or the buildings on it or part thereof, to a third party(s).

The transfer fee for such a land title can be very costly, depending on location and usage. A large portion of this fee will be paid to the State Land Bureau while the rest goes to the municipal or provincial land administration bureau and the county or district land office where the land is located. Since such arrangements are meant mainly for foreigners or Sino-foreign enterprises, contributions for infrastructure, utilities etc., including land related taxes are also relatively higher.

Repatriation of Profits

There are provisions in Chinese law to assure foreign business people of their rights to repatriation of profits:

Article 18 of the "Constitution of the People's Republic of China" stipulates that "the People's Republic of China (PRC) allows foreign enterprises and other economic organizations or individuals to make investments in China and have all forms of economic co-operation with the Chinese enterprise or other economic organization in accordance with the provisions of the laws of PRC. Foreign enterprises and other economic organizations with foreign investments operating within the Chinese territory must abide by the laws of the PRC. Their legitimate rights and interests shall be protected by the laws of the PRC."

Article 5 of the "Detailed Regulations and Rules of Civil Law of the People's Republic of China" stipulates that the "civil rights of the citizens and the legal persons are under the protection of the law. No organization or individual shall violate such rights."

Article 10 of "The Law of the People's Republic of China on Chinese-Foreign Equity Joint Ventures" stipulates that "the share of the net profits of the foreign participants after fulfilling their obligations under the law and the joint venture contract, their capitals obtained at the termination or cancellation of the enterprise and other funds can be remitted abroad in the currency stipulated by the contract through the Bank of China in accordance with the regulations of foreign administration."

Article 3 of "The Law of the People's Republic of China on Chinese-Foreign Contractual Joint Ventures" stipulates that "the State shall, according to the law, protect the lawful rights and interests of the contractual joint ventures and the Chinese and foreign parties."

Article 23 of "The Law of the People's Republic of China on Chinese- Foreign Contractual Joint Ventures" stipulates that "after the foreign party has fulfilled its obligations under the law and the contractual joint venture contract, the profits it receives as its share, its other legitimate income and funds it received as its share upon termination of the venture, may be remitted abroad according to the law. The wages, salaries or other legitimate income earned by the foreign staff and workers of the contractual joint ventures, after the payment of individual income tax accordance to the law, may be remitted abroad."

Article 4 of "The Law of the People's Republic of China on Enterprises Operated Exclusively with Foreign Capital" stipulates that "the investment made by the foreign investors in China, the profits they earn and their other lawful rights and interests shall be protected by Chinese laws. The wholly-owned foreign enterprises must abide by the Chinese laws and statutes and must do nothing detrimental to China's public interests."

Autonomy in Management and Operation

Article 15 of the "Provisions of the State Council for the Encouragement of Foreign Investment" stipulates that "the people's government at all levels and competent departments concerned should provide insurance for the autonomy of the enterprises with foreign investment and positively support them to conduct management with internationally advanced scientific measures. Within the scope of the approved contract, the enterprise with foreign investment enjoys the right to work out their plans of production and management, raise and use funds, buy production material, sell products, determine levels of salaries, forms of salaries and bonuses, subsidy systems, etc. on their own.

"Enterprises with foreign investment may, depending on the needs of production and management, decide the organization and employment and/or removal of staff. The units concerned (basically referring to your local partners) should give positive support and permit the transfer of such employees. Employees, who violate the rules and regulations and hence bring certain bad results, shall be punished or even fired depending on the seriousness of the incident. Enterprises with foreign investment shall report the employment or dismissal of employees, for record purposes, to the local labor and personnel departments."

Article 5 of the "Provisions of Beijing Municipal People's Government for the Encouragement of Foreign Investment" stipulates that "When enterprises with foreign investment recruit personnel from among the staff within the local organizations, the departments and enterprises concerned shall give positive support and allow their own employees to take up such employment. The staff may resign if their original employer (*danwei*) shall put up unjustifiable obstructions. When disputes arise, the parties concerned may apply to the Municipal Personnel Exchange and Service Center and the Municipal Labor Exchange Center may directly handle job transfer formalities for the recruited staff. In case the enterprises with foreign investment dismiss its staff pursuant to the stipulated contracts of relevant provisions, no department, organization or individual has the right to intervene in the affairs of such dismissal."

Be advised though that although these provisions seem quite explicit, when it comes to actual implementation, there can be problems.

CHAPTER 10

The Legal System

The Chinese legal system is a communist system, where everything belongs to the people but is managed by the Central Government under the Standing Committee of the National People's Congress. Essentially, the Communist Party controls the legislature, which, in turn, controls the judiciary.

Prior to 1983, a judge need not be, and in most cases, was not, a legally qualified person. The minimum qualification stipulated was that the person must be at least 23 years of age, have the right to vote and have not been deprived of his or her political privileges.

An amendment to this was made in 1983, which required that a judge have proper knowledge of the law. Professional

Court of Justice

qualifications were omitted, probably because of the lack of qualified persons. Provincial bar examinations for such candidates were cursory. In 1986, more rigid requirements for judges and lawyers were imposed. National law examinations and a minimum requirement for judges and lawyers were introduced.

There are three divisions in the Chinese judicial system: the Public Securities, the People's Procuratorates and the Courts. The Public Securities, under the State Council, comprise three ministries:

- Ministry of Public Security, which takes charge of domestic security including household registration, criminal investigations, traffic control, fire safety and frontier controls.
- Ministry of State Security, which is responsible for control of espionage involving foreign powers.
- Ministry of Justice, which trains lawyers and runs the law schools. It also supervises and regulates lawyers, law firms and notaries and is responsible for enhancing public awareness of the law.

Since the "open door policy," the Central Government has made various changes to put the law in line with international practise and expectations. This has not been easy as there is no suitable model or predecessor. An adaptation of laws from many countries, mainly the United States and the newly industrialized "Southeast Asian Tigers" was made.

The transformation has been a very slow and gradual process, very much by trial and error. Laws and regulations are often termed "provisional or interim" and changed as soon as they are found unsatisfactory. From 1979 to 1992, more than 400 laws and regulations concerning foreign investments were promulgated by the Central Government. Not surprisingly, foreign investors are apprehensive of, if not frustrated by, the constant changes.

Notwithstanding all the efforts to change and bring the system in line with international practise, China's legal system is still greatly influenced by the Chinese Communist Party (CCP) which continues to be the supreme power in all matters, including the courts. This gives rise to the possibility of a legal dispute being resolved on political rather than legal grounds, and bias towards the local party's case. It is probably one reason many foreigners prefer to settle out of court.

Obsession with secrecy among the Chinese also means that many rules and regulations are not published, hence often catching foreign business people unprepared. Uncertainty about Chinese laws and regulations and the fact that legislation is not uniformly applied across the country are the main complaints by foreign business people.

The Chinese legal system originates from, and is sanctioned by, the Central Government in Beijing. The laws are then passed down to the provincial, municipal and other levels of government and modified to serve their particular purpose or interest. They are again adapted at county and district levels.

Unfortunately, the laws and policies set by the Central Government are often distorted in the process. While the principles are normally quite clear, they are often intentionally misinterpreted as local interests come into play. The Chinese call them "counter policies." There is a well-known Chinese saying: *Shang you zheng ce, xia you dui ce.* Literally translated, it means "the top have a policy (or regulation or law), below we have a counter policy." This precisely describes the attitude of some Chinese officials towards their laws and regulations. They always look for ways to manipulate the system and promote their interests.

Another commonly heard phrase is shan *gao huang di yuan* — the mountain is high and the King is far away, that is, the Central Government is too far away to have any effective control over the local officials. Apparently the phrase originated in Guangzhou where the laws and regulations are considered most "flexible" because of its distance from the Central Government in Beijing. By contrast, Beijing, because of its proximity to the Central

Beating the System
We were trying to seek the advise and help of the chief of the tax bureau of a certain province and therefore invited him to dinner. At that time, the Central Government had just launched a campaign to purge corruption. There was a lot of publicity on the anti-graft campaign and an apparent restriction that officials of his status should not accept invitations by foreigners to unofficial functions. Because of this, he had to turn down our invitation.

Coincidentally, his spouse was our business associate. We approached her and her advise was quite simple. We should invite the wife to dinner instead and at the same time request his company. He would then be "merely accompanying his spouse to dinner." We did just that. He attended the dinner but had to give up the guest of honor seat to his wife. However, we had a very fruitful discussion and achieved our objective.

Government, is known to be very rigid in its enforcement of its laws and regulations.

Rapid developments in China in the last two decades have made it difficult for legislators to cope with the changes. This is compounded by the lack of trained people who understand and can implement and administer the law. It is quite common to find middle-level officials in the rural areas who do not fully understand their roles in office, and magistrates and county chiefs who were farmers.

To overcome the problems, the Central Government has printed legislation, standard forms, contracts of various types and even models for various applications. It is mandatory to use the standard forms, which have to be purchased from the relevant authorities, for all contracts. Although the use of these standard forms is mandatory, you can attach amendments to the terms and conditions stated in the standard forms. There have been instances where the attachments void the terms and conditions in the standard form but were accepted because they were submitted with the standard form.

The Chinese Judicial System

At the top of the judicial system is the Supreme People's Courts followed by the High Courts, the Intermediate Courts and the Basic Courts. These courts are divided into tribunals handling criminal, civil, commercial and other administrative cases. A single judge handles simple civil disputes and minor criminal cases. For others, a panel comprising an odd number of judges similar to the jury system will preside. The jurors do not pass judgment. They merely make recommendations on the hearing. A judicial committee passes judgment.

The judicial committee consists of a Chairman, a President of the Court and various other members. The local People's Congress elects the President of the Court at each respective level and approves the selection of its members. However, it is the Communist Party Committee which appoints its Chairman who in turn nominates the members. The judicial process can therefore be described as a series of formalities where a collective decision is then made. The President of the Court signs and stamps all judgments, but it is quite clear that the power lies in the hands of the Communist Party via the Chairman of the judicial committee.

Commercial and corporate laws are relatively new in China as a proper legal system was instituted only after the economic reform policy was adopted and China opened up to the outside world. Much fine-tuning is still necessary. Because of this, legal redress is normally quite difficult and often a long-drawn affair.

Arbitration

As an integral part of its reform, China has set up the China International Economic & Trade Arbitration Commission (CIETAC). This panel of sixty-five arbitrators, of whom nine are foreign experts appointed by the Government, enjoys a fairly good reputation for greater competence and impartiality than the courts.

According to the Arbitration Law adopted by the National People's Congress on 31 August 1994, the arbitration awards are final and neither party may appeal to the courts. Arbitration is normally the preferred course of action in a dispute in China because:

- there is less acrimony and the contending parties need not necessarily break up. In many instances, they may still continue their business together.
- arbitration can be done anywhere in the world subject to the agreement of both parties, whereas litigation concerning a contract signed in China can only be done in China.
- there is greater flexibility than in litigation.

Laws on Foreign-Capital Enterprises
(Promulgated by Order No 39 of the President of the People's Republic of China and effective from 12 April 1986)

Article 1
With a view to expanding economic co-operation and technical exchange with foreign countries and promoting the development of China's national economy, the People's Republic of China permits foreign enterprises, and other foreign economic organizations and individuals (hereinafter collectively referred to as "foreign investors") to set up enterprises with foreign capital in China, and protects the lawful rights and interests of such enterprises.

Article 2
As mentioned in this law, "enterprises with foreign capital" refers to those enterprises established in China by foreign investors, exclusively with their own capital, in accordance with the relevant Chinese laws. The term does not include branches set up in China by foreign enterprises and other foreign economic organizations.

Article 3

Enterprises with foreign capital shall be established in such a manner as to help the development of China's national economy; they shall use advanced technology and equipment or market all or most of their products outside China. Provisions shall be made by the State Council regarding the lines of business which the State forbids enterprises with foreign capital to engage in or on which it places certain restrictions.

Article 4

The investments of a foreign investor in China, the profits earned and its other lawful rights and interests are protected by Chinese law. Enterprises with foreign capital must abide by Chinese laws and regulations and must not engage in any activity detrimental to China's public interest.

Article 5

The State shall not nationalize or requisition any enterprise with foreign capital. Under special circumstances, when public interest requires, enterprises with foreign capital may be requisitioned by legal procedures and appropriate compensation shall be made.

Article 6

The application to establish an enterprise with foreign capital shall be submitted for examination and approval to the department under the State Council, which is in charge of foreign economic relations and trade, or to another agency authorized by the State Council. The authorities in charge of examination and approval shall, within 90 days from the date they receive such application, decide whether or not to grant approval.

Article 7

After an application for the establishment of an enterprise with foreign capital has been approved, the foreign investor shall, within

30 days from the date of receiving a certificate of approval, apply to the Industry and Commerce Administration authorities for registration and obtain a business license. The date of issue of the business license shall be the date of the establishment of the enterprise.

Article 8
An enterprise with foreign capital, which meets the conditions for being considered a legal person under Chinese law, shall acquire the status of a Chinese legal person, in accordance with the law.

Article 9
An enterprise with foreign capital shall make investments in China within the period approved by the authorities in charge of examination and approval. If it fails to do so, the industry and commerce administration authorities may cancel its business license. The Industry and Commerce Administration authorities shall inspect and supervise the investment situation of an enterprise with foreign capital.

Article 10
In the event of a separation, merger or other major change, an enterprise with foreign capital shall report to, and seek approval from, the authorities in charge of examination and approval, and register the change with the Industry and Commerce Administration authorities.

Article 11
The production and operating plans of enterprises with foreign capital shall be reported to the competent authorities for the record. Enterprises with foreign capital shall conduct their operations and management in accordance with the approved articles of association, and shall be free from any interference.

Article 12

When employing Chinese workers and staff, an enterprise with foreign capital shall conclude contracts with them according to law, in which matters concerning employment, dismissal, remuneration, welfare benefits, labor protection and labor insurance shall be clearly prescribed.

Article 13

Workers and staff in enterprises with foreign capital may organise trade unions in accordance with the law, in order to conduct trade union activities and protect their lawful rights and interests. The enterprise shall provide the necessary conditions for the activities of the trade unions in their respective enterprises.

Article 14

An enterprise with foreign capital must set up account books in China, conduct independent accounting, submit the fiscal reports and statements as required and accept supervision by the financial and tax authorities. If an enterprise with foreign capital refuses to maintain account books in China, the financial and tax authorities may impose a fine on it, and the Industry and Commerce Administration authorities may order it to suspend operations or may revoke its business license.

Article 15

Within the scope of the operations approved, an enterprise with foreign capital may purchase, either in China or from the world market, raw and semi-processed materials, and fuels and other materials they need. When these materials are available from both sources on similar terms, first priority should be given to purchases in China.

Article 16
Enterprises with foreign capital shall apply to insurance companies in China for such kinds of insurance coverage as are needed.

Article 17
Enterprises with foreign capital shall pay taxes in accordance with relevant state provisions for tax payment, and may enjoy preferential treatment for reduction or exemption from taxes. An enterprise that reinvests its profits in China after paying the income tax, may in accordance with relevant state provisions, apply for refund of a part of the income tax already paid on the reinvested amount.

Article 18
Enterprises with foreign capital shall handle their foreign exchange transactions in accordance with the state provisions for foreign exchange control. Enterprises with foreign capital shall manage to balance their own foreign exchange receipts and payments. If, with the approval of the competent authorities, the enterprises market their products in China and consequently experience an imbalance in foreign exchange, the said authorities shall help them correct the imbalance.

Article 19
The foreign investor may remit abroad profits that are lawfully earned from an enterprise with foreign capital, as well as other lawful earnings and any funds remaining after the enterprise is liquidated. Wages, salaries and other legitimate income earned by foreign employees in an enterprise with foreign capital may be remitted abroad after the payment of individual income tax in accordance with the law.

Article 20

With respect to the period of operations of an enterprise with foreign capital, the foreign investor shall report to and secure approval from the authorities in charge of examination and approval. For an extension of the period of operations, an application shall be submitted to the said authorities 180 days before the expiration of the period. The authorities in charge of examination and approval shall, within 30 days from the date such application is received, decide whether or not to grant the extension.

Article 21

When terminating its operations, an enterprise with foreign capital shall promptly issue a public notice and proceed with liquidation in accordance with legal procedure. Pending the completion of liquidation, a foreign investor may not dispose of the assets of the enterprise except for the purpose of liquidation.

Article 22

At the termination of operations, the enterprise with foreign capital shall nullify its registration with the Industry and Commerce Administration authorities and hand in its business license for cancellation.

Article 23

The department under the State Council which is in charge of foreign economic relations and trade shall, in accordance with this Law, formulate rules for its implementation, which shall go into effect after being submitted to and approved by the State Council.

Article 24

This Law shall go into effect on the day of its promulgation.

Some of the main features in the investment laws for foreign capital enterprises are:

Equity Joint Ventures (1979)

1 The foreign portion of the joint venture must be at least 25% of the capital investment.
2 The profit and risk or liability shall be shared proportionately to the investment ratio.
3 The regulated equity-debt ratio are:
   • if the registered capital and total investment is below US$30 million—40%, and
   • for investments above US$30 million—33%
4 The period of joint ventures is 10 years to 30 years but may vary depending on the type of joint ventures and investment involved.
5 The foreign capital enterprises are required to maintain a foreign exchange balance.
6 Certain limitations are imposed on:
   • access to sales in the China market, and
   • priority on local material

In 1986 and 1990, some amendments were made to include:
• No nationalization may take place, but if it is required for public interest, then appropriate compensation has to be paid.
• Foreigners may also serve as Chairman of the Board of Directors.
• With mutual consent and approval, the joint venture may extend its original term of operation.
• The joint venture may also bank at any approved foreign exchange institution.

Co-operative/Contractual Joint Venture (1988)

1 No restriction on percentage of foreign capital
2 Share of profit and liability shall be by contract. No restriction by law.
3 Period of contract—no restriction.
4 Balance of foreign exchange receipts required.
5 May opt to be a limited liability entity.

Wholly Foreign-owned Enterprise (1986)

1 Restricted to advanced technology and equipment or fully export-oriented products.
2 Non-interference is to be the rule for submission of production and operational plans to government "for record".
3 50% maximum tax.
4 Chinese insurance required.
5 Priority to local sourcing on competitive terms.
6 Foreign exchange account must be balanced.
7 General supervision by approving authorities.

Summary of Major Laws and Regulations Concerning Foreign Investment

1979 Equity Joint Venture Law

1980 **Procedures for Registration of Joint Ventures**
  — Regulations on Labor Management of Joint Ventures
  — Foreign Exchange Control
  — Regulations on Representative Office for Foreign Enterprise
  — Import & Export Licensing Procedures
  — Individual Income Tax Law
  — Guangdong SEZs Regulation

1981 **Procedure for Loan to Joint Ventures by Bank of China**
  — Income Tax Law for Joint Ventures
  — Contract Laws

1982 **Trademark Laws**

1983 **Arbitration Laws & Regulations**
  — Regulations for Property Insurance
  — Regulations & Laws for Equity Joint Ventures
  — Law on Statistics

1984 **Inspection Regulations for Import & Export**
  — Patent Law
  — Special Tax Incentives for the 14 Coastal Economic and Technological Development Zones
  — Regulations on Foreign Ownership of Private Property

1985 **Import & Export Tariff**
  — Law of Contracts involving Foreign Interest
  — Regulations on Foreign & Joint Venture Banks in the Special Economic Zones
  — Regulations on Import of Technology
  — Laws on Entry & Exit of Foreigners

1986 Foreign Exchange Control
— Laws on Wholly Foreign-owned Enterprises
— Provisions for Encouragement of Foreign Investment
— Regulations on Employment, Wages & Welfare in Joint Ventures
— Customs Regulations

1987 Customs Laws
— Regulations on Registered Capital in Joint Ventures
— Revision in Regulations of Equity Joint Ventures
— Regulations on Investment Contribution of Joint Venture Partners

1988 Laws on Contractual Joint Venture
— Regulation on Incentives to Develop Hainan Island
— Regulations on Expansion of Coastal Economic Zones
— Regulations on Free Trade Zones & Bonded Warehouse
— Land Control Laws
— Auditing Regulations
— State Council Decision on Expanding Provincial Approving Authority for Joint Ventures

1989 Regulations on Foreign Chambers of Commerce in China
— Regulations on Foreign-related Notary

1990 Regulations on Tenure for Joint Ventures
— Laws on Wholly Foreign-owned Enterprises
— Revisions on Laws of Equity Joint Ventures
— Copyright Laws
— Regulation on Computer Software Protection
— Incentives for Shanghai Pudong New Development Zones
— Regulations on Foreign Land Developers

1991 Land Management Laws
— Regulations on New and High-technological
Development Zones
— Corporate Income Tax Law for Joint Ventures
— Copyright Laws

1992

— Revision for Patent Laws
— State Council Decision to Open More Border Towns
— Laws on Limited Liability Companies
— Regulations on Incorporated Shareholding
Companies
— Regulations on Accounting & Fiscal Management
for Joint Ventures

1993 Revision on Contract Laws
— Law on Unfair Competition

CHAPTER 11

Taxes

In 1994, a new taxation system was announced to be applied throughout China. The total restructuring of its commercial and industrial taxation system was to adapt it to the market economy, in line with international tax systems and practises.

Types of Taxes
There are various forms of taxes in China.

Foreign Enterprise Income Tax (FEIT)
All foreign enterprises carrying out business in China are subjected to an FEIT at a flat rate of 30%, plus a 3% local tax on the taxable profit.

Tax Incentives
The tax incentives are 15% for the five Special Economic Zones (in Shenzhen, Zhuhai, Xiamen, Shantou and Hainan Island) and 24% for the fourteen Coastal Cities Open Economic Zones and other designated areas.

There is a two-year tax holiday plus three years of 50% reduction for production enterprises operating for at least five years. The tax holidays commence from the first profit-making year, and cannot be deferred once started.

There are special tax holidays/rates for infrastructure projects.

Advanced technology enterprises enjoy a further 50% reduction for a further three years after the expiration of the normal tax holidays.

Export enterprises can also enjoy a 50% reduction for a further three years after the expiration of the normal tax holidays, if they export more than 70% of their total products.

Tax Refund for Reinvestment

Foreign investors can get a tax refund of 40% of the tax paid on their reinvested profits under the following conditions:

- undistributed profits are reinvested to increase the registered capital of the existing company, operational for a minimum period of five years
- shares of profit are reinvested in another Foreign Investment Enterprise, operational for a minimum period of five years
- if an export or technologically-advanced enterprise is expanded or established, there may be a 100% refund on the tax paid on the reinvested amount

Withholding Tax

The standard rate is at 20%, with a reduced rate of 10% for Special Economic Zones (SEZ) and other designated zones.

For income on interest, there is a reduction to 10% for loan agreement concluded before 31 December 1995. There is no withholding tax on dividends.

Value Added Tax (VAT)

Value Added Tax is levied on sales of goods, provision of services and importation of goods. The VAT for most goods and services is around 17%, and 13% for food and basic necessities.

Business Tax

Business tax is levied on taxable services including construction, transportation, finance, insurance, communication, education, and entertainment. Business tax is also applicable to the transfer of immovable and intangible property in China. For all other services except processing and repairs services, transfer of tangibles and real estate property, the tax rates varies from 3% to 20% (for an entertainment business, it can be as high as 20%).

Consumption Tax

Consumption tax is levied on the production and import of certain products.

Customs Duty (CD)

Customs duty is levied on the Carriage, Insurance and Freight (CIF) value of import. The duties vary depending on the type of product imported.

Customs duty may be exempted:

- when equipment and machinery imported by the foreign enterprise is within its total investments in China
- when raw materials, ancillary material, components, parts and other materials are imported specially for production of goods for export
- for export sales, except crude oil and chemical products specified by the Chinese authorities

Customs Building

In the import of automobiles, VAT and customs duty are payable even if they are part of the total investment.

Stamp Duty
Stamp duty is payable on all dutiable documents, such as contracts, Deed of Transfer of Property, permits, licenses.

Real Estate Tax (RET)
RET is paid by the owner/mortgagee of the real estate based on the value of the estate, and it varies between the cities in China. It ranges from 1% to 5% and is determined by the local authority. Exemptions are allowed for properties owned by individuals which are not used for business. RET is assessed on an annual basis but payable in installments.

Land Appreciation Tax
Applicable on capital gains derived from sale or transfer of property and/or land use rights but not applicable for transfer of real estate by way of inheritance or gift. The tax rate varies from 30% to 60%.

Land Use Tax
Tax on the use of the land, whether for residential, commercial, industrial or agricultural. purposes. The tax rate varies according to the locality and city. It ranges from RMB2 to RMB8 per sq m for industrial land in the outskirts and up to RMB150 per sq m for commercial property in the cities.

Urban Maintenance and Construction Tax
This tax is levied on enterprises at about 0.5% to 2% of the business tax.

Vehicle & Vessel License Tax
Tax is levied according to type of vehicle and tonnage.

Preferential Tax Policies for Industrial Development
Category/Type of Industry

- **Enterprise Income Tax**
  Manufacturing enterprises operating 10 years
  > first and second profit-making years: tax exempted
  > third and subsequent years: 50% reduction

- Foreign export-oriented enterprises exporting 70% or more of its annual output
  > first and second profit-making years: tax exempted
  > third to fifth year: 50% reduction
  > subsequent years: 50% reduction (subject to min. 10% tax)

- Technologically advanced enterprises
  > first and second profit-making years: tax exempted
  > third to eighth year: 50% reduction

- Foreign enterprises engaged in technology-intensive projects: 15%

- Foreign manufacturing enterprises with investments of more than US$30 million and a long payback period: 15%

- Foreign enterprises engaged in harbor or wharf construction operating at least 15 years
  > first to fifth year: tax exempted
  > sixth to tenth year: 50% reduction

- Dividends, rental, royalties: 10%

- Reinvestment of profits for a period of five years or more by the foreign enterprises: 40% or full rebate

Note: The above do not apply to all developments and varies from city to city.

Double Taxation Treaties

The People's Republic of China has double taxation treaties with the following countries:

Australia, Belgium, Bulgaria, Canada, Cyprus, Czechoslovakia, Denmark, Finland, France, Germany, Italy, Japan, Kuwait, Malaysia, Netherlands, New Zealand, Norway, Pakistan, Poland, Singapore, Spain, Sweden, Switzerland, Thailand, United Kingdom, the United States and Yugoslavia.

Individual Income Tax (IIT)

The New Individual Income Tax Regulations, effective from 1 January 1994, is applicable to all foreigners and locals.

Application

All Chinese citizens are levied an Individual Income Tax on their worldwide income. For foreign business people, this tax is levied on their income derived from the People's Republic of China.

Double taxation treaties apply if the total stay in China does not exceed 183 days.

Taxable Income

All cash and non-cash payments are taxable. These include salaries, wages, royalties, interests, dividends and bonuses, rentals, leasing charges, income from transfer of properties and windfall gains.

Non-cash benefits are, in practise, not taxed. These include free housing, use of company car, reimbursement of meals and living expenses. They are treated as business expenses.

Worldwide Income

Individual Income Tax is levied on all Chinese residents on their worldwide income, and non-residents on all income derived from within China. A limited exception applies to non-residents who have been in China for fewer than 90 days.

Foreigners working full time in China and/or having "Resident Permit of China" are subjected to the same tax law. The new tax rates range from 5% to 45% of all wages, and 5% to 35% for an individually-owned business.

A flat rate of 20% is levied on other income derived from professional writing, professional fees for personal services, consultancy, royalty, interest, dividends, bonuses, leases, transfer of property, incidental income, etc.

Employers are responsible for ensuring that their employees, suppliers, contractors and organizations providing services of any sort to them, pay their taxes. In order to ensure this, the employers are given the right to withhold taxes payable by such employees or organization. Generally the withholding tax is 20% flat. A handling fee of 2% of the tax amount withheld is paid to the withholding agent.

CHAPTER 12

Venturing into China

Most foreign business people venture into China because of the enormous market and cheap labor provided by the nearly 1.3 billion people. China encourages export-oriented investment and many incentives are given to these investors. You will need an approved project and a Chinese partner. You can source for projects and/or partners through:

(a) Agents or government and local authorities

Government agencies, private agencies and private individuals are permitted under Chinese laws to charge and collect agency fees for such introductions. This is about 1% to 3%, but can also vary from 0.5% to 5% depending on the situation and terms of reference. Be aware that many agents or authorities are only interested in closing the deal so that they can collect their commission. Therefore check all details.

If you have a product or business on the priority list of businesses, you may apply directly to the Ministry of Foreign Trade and Economic Co-operation (MOFTEC) which will recommend business partners to you. Again, a good relationship with the MOFTEC officials means good recommendations.

(b) Contact and/or recommendation by high officials

Ministers, party secretaries, and mayors usually have a list of partners or projects, if you have the network to reach them. Acquiring a project in this manner immediately gives you a high profile because it means that you have connections (*guanxi*) at the top. This definitely eases your way through many problems. However, do not ignore those at the operational level. There is a well-known Chinese saying: *bu pa guan, zi pa kuan*, meaning, "there is no need to fear the high officials, but one has to be wary of the person directly supervising and/or in control of one's business or project."

If you are referred to MOFTEC, the quality of the organization recommended to you depends on the rank of the official you know or the official who attended to your application.

Projects
China encourages foreign investments in:
- infrastructure projects involving huge investments
- primary industries
- high-technology industries
- export-oriented industries.

A mega project by Li Ka Shing

Conditions vary for each type of investment, so it is important to check everything in detail before commitment to a project. The rule for foreign business people here is not to take anything for granted. Have all the conditions in writing whenever and wherever possible. Conduct a separate feasibility study of the proposed project and compare the information with the information supplied to you by your local partner(s).

Different Interpretations

A friend was involved in a negotiation for a B.O.T. (build, operate and transfer) project to build an expressway from a nearby county to Beijing. Volumes of data were provided by the Chinese authorities. These included the daily traffic volume on the existing road and the volume per month. Based on the data provided, the project seemed extremely profitable and his Board of Directors was very excited. He was instructed by his directors to sign the agreement as soon as possible.

When he spoke to me about the project, my experience warned me that it was too good to be true. We decided to check the information out.

Through a local associate, we got to know the junior engineer responsible for the survey and compilation of the data in that road department. From the breakdown given by this engineer, we realized that, apart from normal traffic like cars and lorries, that particular stretch of road was heavily used by carts driven by horses, donkeys, bulls and even people. The numbers given for the "traffic" flow included all these except bicycles. The data was therefore misleading.

When confronted, the Chinese officials reacted angrily. They argued that the information was correct and that the word "traffic" included all kinds of vehicles except bicycles. They further argued that the B.O.T. operator could still charge a toll on horse-carts and all other vehicles.

The new data showed that the project was no longer feasible and it was eventually abandoned.

Choosing a Location

Proximity to the following should be considered:

- central business districts or town centers
- transportation network (air, sea and land)
- resources (raw materials, manpower and information)
- market (whether local or international)
- infrastructure and utilities

Central Business Districts/Town Centers

Depending on the size and stage of development, a town center or business district in one province can be very different in another. For example, the suburban town centre in Xujiahui, Shanghai, is many times more developed and vibrant compared to Hefei, the city center of Anhui, which is a province adjacent to the Jiangsu province. Therefore, do not immediately sign on the dotted line when you are offered a piece of land in "the heart of the city center" for a price of one tenth that of Shanghai. Check it out first.

Transportation

Air   Many international airlines fly to the main coastal cities in China. The Civil Aviation Administration of China (CAAC), with its many domestic airlines, provides domestic flights between the cities and on several other international routes. Despite the rapid expansion program, there is still a severe shortage of seats. Air cargo space is also heavily booked.

There are many flights between the major cities in China but in some of the smaller cities, because of the limited number of flights available in a week, you may have to wait for as long as a week to get onto another flight if you miss one. Scarcity creates opportunity for corruption. Very often, purchasing a ticket in these cities requires *guanxi* or under-the-table payments.

Sea   China has about 126 large ports along its coastline and inland waterways. Of these, fifteen handle international trade.

The port of Shanghai is China's most important and largest port. Although Dalian is the second largest, it handles far less foreign trade than Tianjin. While the port of Guangzhou is important for trade in China, it has been used less for international trade because of its proximity to Hong Kong. The port in Hong Kong handles about 90 percent of all China's container trade.

Land   Trains still provide the main means of transport for most people on their inter-city journeys. They are also the main and most efficient means of transporting goods between cities, and their schedules are normally quite accurate.

The trains are normally overcrowded. During peak periods, you may even see passengers climbing into the trains through the windows instead of the doors in their rush for seats. There are generally two classes of passenger seats or compartments. The "hard seats" are for the common people and the fare is extremely cheap. Tickets are reserved for locals only.

The "soft seats" class is reserved for foreigners and senior cadres and is quite comfortable. There are also sleeping berths. The compartments and bedding are very basic but fairly clean. Normally, there are four berths in a compartment. If you travel alone, you may have to share with three other passengers.

Lorries and trucks are commonly used for transportation of goods in journeys of not more than two or three days.

Resources
Raw materials   Proximity to sources of raw materials and ports must be taken into account because of the transportation problems in China.

Manpower You will find skilled and trained personnel more easily in major cities, but wages will be higher. Cheap unskilled labor is plentiful in smaller cities and rural areas.

Information   Due to the poor transport and communication system, availability of information is a big problem in China. For example, *China Daily*, China's only English language national newspaper, is available in Beijing and in Shanghai on the same day as the date printed on it. However, if you are in Wuhan or Qingdao, you get it three days late. Outside of Beijing and Shanghai, it is extremely difficult to get any international newspapers that are less than four days old. Of course, telecommunications and the internet are now alternatives but do bear in mind that these services are only available in some of the more developed cities.

Market
If you are looking at a local market where distribution of goods to other cities is required, check out the inland distribution network. If you are looking at an international market, consider proximity to ports and airports.

Infrastructure and Utilities
Check that the necessary infrastructure and utilities are available, especially in smaller cities. Even in the bigger and more developed cities, the infrastructure and utilities system may be overstretched because of the rapid economic development and expansion.

Take note that what is "more than sufficient" to the Chinese may not be enough for your needs.

Getting a Chinese Business Partner
Your Chinese business partner will be from private enterprises or the state-owned enterprises.

Not all Chinese organizations are allowed to sign contracts with foreigners. These include the self-employed, family-owned businesses, and mass organizations like trade unions, institutions and government departments funded by the State unless they are companies registered with the Administration for Industry and Commerce as independent business organizations.

The importance of getting a good partner cannot be overemphasized. It can determine the success of your partnership and the profitability of the venture. For large projects or investments, political connections at local, provincial and, where possible, State levels are useful. Training is often required. Keep in mind the totally different cultural, political and economic background of your Chinese business partner. Understanding the business culture and mindset will work in your interest.

Remember that in the unfortunate event of a dispute, seeking redress in China through legal channels is difficult and often a long-drawn and unfruitful process. Establishing and maintaining a good relationship with your partner is therefore very important.

In general, the officials (including the Party Secretaries, and Mayors) in China are appointed on a five-year term. Reviews are made every five years and such officials may either retain their jobs/positions, be promoted or be transferred laterally to another company or *danwei*. This is evident in your joint venture contract and/or memorandum of association where the appointment of Chairman, Directors and General Manager is on a five-year term.

Hard currency funding can be a problem for many Chinese enterprises. Very often, they depend on the foreign investors to fund the project. It is therefore important to check whether your potential partner has access to the funding required in your joint endeavor.

As your local partner(s) will probably be from one of the state-owned enterprises, a government or quasi-government organization, when a relationship fails, they may claim to represent China's investment or even the Chinese government and you may find yourself in a dispute against the interest of "China's investment or even the Chinese Government."

Your relationship with your partner(s) is therefore important. It is prudent to establish a good relationship with the key personnel in your partner's organization and those appointed as Directors and/or holding key positions in your joint venture company.

In China, the communist party and party cadres still command a lot of power in the state-owned enterprises and, in any dispute, they have the last word. A good working relationship and the support of even people with whom you do not have direct dealings with, is important.

At the same time, the Chinese are always eager to work well with foreign business people, sometimes even at the expense of their own organization or the State. This is in their interest because, with a foreign partner, they and their whole organization, will receive better benefits, both tangible and intangible.

Why you would Need a Chinese Business Partner

Most foreign investments in China are joint ventures as there are several areas where having local business partners can be useful. Some of the advantages that they bring with them include:

- facilitating and reducing local administrative problems
- local knowledge of the product or services that you are investing in.
- *guanxi* or connections for your venture
- lowering your initial capital investment in land, premises, equipment, market and other assets
- cheaper labor costs as labor costs are much lower in local enterprises. This is more so if it is a joint venture with a state-owned enterprise, but look out for hidden costs.
- use of the partner's business license as foreigners are restricted from operating certain businesses.

Take note that having controlling shares in a joint venture does not always mean that you have the final say. In China, a local business partner with minority shares can create awkward situations.

Negotiating for a Project

Sometimes, you may find yourself negotiating with agents or a third party instead of the real party involved in the proposed venture. This is quite common in China. These intermediaries will normally highlight the "extras" that you must consider apart from the official terms and conditions in your negotiation. These "extras" are supposed to get you better terms on the official front but it will not be raised directly by your potential partner(s). However, it is essential that before you start the actual negotiation, you should check and ensure that the person you are talking to is authorized to participate and/or act as intermediary on whatever agreement you are negotiating.

Important Points to Remember

Agreement not Binding unless Approved by Authorities

Remember that your joint venture contract is legally binding only after the relevant authorities have approved it and not when the agreement is signed. Under normal circumstances, the authorities will not revoke your signed contract. However, do remember that they can if they wish to. Of course this would be with valid reasons to justify the rejection.

Audit of Accounts

Always get professional help for this purpose, including valuation of assets and liabilities.

Statements of Accounts

Do not accept the Statements of Accounts prepared by your local partner solely for the purpose of the joint venture negotiation, at face value. Check the accounting principles used, method of valuation and also past performance. It is advisable to always check the past performance and if there is more than one set of accounts.

Changing Conditions
The foreign investors of an industrial park project thought that they had a very good deal purchasing land at RMB15,000 per *mu* (Chinese acre) when they were told by their local business partner that the market value should be about RMB30,000. The local Land Office, which is also the only authorized party to do a valuation at this place, valued the land at about RMB25,000 per *mu*.

A year later, after the investors had paid for the land, more land around the first piece, and with similar conditions, was offered to other investors at only RMB10,000 a *mu*.

This illustrates either that the method of valuation is incomprehensible or that even an official valuation can be manipulated to attract foreign investment.

In this case, as the vendor was the Government District Officer and the valuation was done by the District Land Office, many would accept the information as authentic and correct. The foreign investors were very upset. However, their Chinese partner argued that the timing and conditions had changed the valuation.

Make sure that the valuation and professional advice you receive is not from an interested party.

Hidden Cost of Retirees and Redundant Workers

The cost of redundant workers, retirees and other committed liabilities within the organization may sometimes not be reflected in the accounts or other reports. Redundant workers and retirees, or what the Chinese call *baofu* which literally means "burden," can be a major cost in some organizations. These redundant workers or retirees are still on the companies' payroll because of the communist "cradle to grave" employment policy.

This is normally not a major problem in new companies. However, for older companies, their *baofu* or retirees and redundant workers may be as much as 30% of the total labor cost.

Valuation of Property

There is a big difference between property set aside for local use and property available to foreigners. Land assigned to state-owned companies is not transferable and is therefore of much lower value. Most (if not all) local organizations or *danwei* in China possess the "rights of use" for the land assigned to them by the local government.

Such land assigned to their local partners can still be used for Sino-foreign joint ventures, but not for real estate development. Prices for this type of land are very much cheaper. It is important to note that you do not own the land and therefore cannot transfer or sell any building or structure or part thereof on this land to a third party.

Since the land belongs to the local government, any building you may have on it will be treated like any state-owned property in any redevelopment or repossession exercise.

Ownership or Land Title can be obtained by paying a land transfer fee. Such fee, which is over and above the "rights of use" fee for the land, will depend very much on the locality and usage of the land. A large portion of this fee will be paid to the State Land Bureau, while the balance will be retained by the local Land Office. Land Titles are issued by the State Land Bureau or via the local Land Office in the form of a certificate bound with a red padded cover called the *hongben* or red book.

Another important point to note is that any property sold to foreigners is subjected to an additional tax or property transfer fee. The current fee is 15% and depends on the type of property involved.

Termination of Partnership

Termination of partnership may occur because of disputes or upon the expiry of the joint venture agreement. Officially, the maximum period for any commercial joint venture is 30 years. It is important to note that on such termination, all immovable assets automatically belong to the Chinese partner. It is therefore important that division of assets on termination of partnership be agreed upon and clearly documented right at the beginning of any joint venture agreement.

China is Ruled by the People and not by Laws

There is a common saying among the Chinese that China is ruled "by the people and not by laws" (*ren zhi bu shi fa zi*). Knowing the right people or *guanxi* gets you around many problems, including legal ones.

Personal relationship is more important in China than inter-corporate relations. Companies will have a good and long business relationship if their key personnel get on well together.

Self-Interest Comes First

Since Chinese officials are government employees, profitability is not their main concern. Personal benefits normally take precedence over the company's interests.

Officials Appointed on Five-year Terms

Several implications of this policy are:

- You cannot expect your Chinese partner's vision to be long-term. It has been said that generally their "modus operandi" is to achieve the most for themselves (not the company) out of their five-year terms.
- There can also be a tendency to protect one's position through not taking any action on issues other than the normal or routine. This is in line with the communist ideology that "if there is no action, there can be no mistake." Under the communist system, punishment for mistakes can be quite severe but reward for good work is very meagre and often insignificant. Actions beyond the "routine" are therefore normally taken only if personal gains like a promotion or benefits are received.

Self before Company

A General Manager of a trading company had a huge stockpile of steel bars. These were purchased at a very high price when he first joined the company. Although the price of steel bars depreciated and was expected to depreciate further by yet another 10% to 20% over the next few months, he held on to the stockpile. His five-year term was due to expire and he had already been informed that he would be transferred to another organization. In his set of accounts, the stock was still valued at the purchase price, even though the actual value had depreciated by almost 20%. In spite of the fact that he knew that a further fall in prices was imminent, he did not sell to cut losses.

His reasons? If he holds on to the stocks, the losses incurred will not be exposed until he is safe in his new position. That would give him another five-year term of peace and comfort in his new company. On the other hand, if he were to sell the stocks to cut losses, his set of accounts would immediately reflect the losses incurred. This would jeopardize his transfer and position in the new organization.

Sharing the Benefits

In foreign joint venture hotels where the Chinese parties assign directors to "supervise" the foreign hotel management, it is the norm for senior cadres in the *danwei* to take turns "enjoying the benefits" of being a director when the directors are changed every two to five years. With the new Director, suppliers and sub-contracting agreements for the hotel will inevitably change. It does not matter how good and competitive the existing suppliers or contractors are. What is important is that the Director must "know these suppliers and sub-contractors well". In most instances, these new arrangements are through *guanxi* brought in by the new Directors..

CHAPTER 13

Setting Up in China

Procedures and Documentation

To start a company, other than a representative office, in China, you must submit an application to the local authorities at the place where the company is to be set up. For the application to be considered, you must have a project, which should be in line with the industrial development of China, and a Chinese partner.

The local authorities, whether at district, county, city, municipal or provincial level, are authorised to act for the Ministry of Foreign Trade and Economic Co-operation (MOFTEC) or *jingmaobu*. The approval limit of these local authorities varies. For larger and certain sensitive projects, approval from the MOFTEC head office is required.

The parties entering into a joint venture can be a company, an enterprise or any other economic organization, or a registered legal entity in the eyes of the Chinese law. The Chinese Communist Party, trade unions and other government organizations, unless separately registered as an economic entity, and all Chinese individuals, cannot be a party to a joint venture. The foreign party may, however, be an economic entity or an individual. It must be noted that under Chinese law, individuals in China are non-legal entities. Sole proprietorship is therefore non-existent in China.

Intention of Co-operation

Foreign investors and their Chinese partners must sign a Letter of Intent or Memorandum of Understanding (LOI or MOU) indicating an intention to negotiate the proposed project. It should be noted that this is not binding in the eyes of the law and, very often, more than one MOU is signed for each proposed project.

Favorable terms offered by one prospective partner are sometimes used by the Chinese to bargain for a better deal from another. Notwithstanding this, the signing of the Letter of Intent or Memorandum of Understanding is the first step in your application to start a company.

Feasibility Study

After signing the Letter of Intent or Memorandum of Understanding, your Chinese partner has to prepare and submit a project proposal and feasibility report to the relevant authorities according to the Letter of Intent signed by the parties. This preliminary feasibility report will have to show that the proposed project/operation is financially and technically feasible. Although it has also to fit in with their national and local priorities, this condition is not taken seriously.

Documents to be prepared and submitted by your Chinese partner include:

- application for examination and approval of the project proposal
- letter of intent
- proposed investment sum for the project
- trade classification of product by the relevant department
- copy of business license of the venture parties
- bank references of the foreign investor

Your Chinese counterpart may prepare an overly optimistic proposal to get approval. Whatever it is, make sure that you know the actual figures. It is a good idea to ask your partner for a written statement of all costs.

Application for Registration of Name of Enterprise

After receiving approval of the project proposal and before the signing of the Contract and Articles of Association, the name of the business must be registered with the Beijing Administration of Industry and Commerce and the following documents submitted in duplicate:

- application signed by the person responsible for the project who is referred to as the "legal representative of the company"
- project proposal and approval documents
- copy of business license

More documentation follows, and a feasibility report must be prepared by both the foreign and Chinese partners for submission to the approving authorities. The documents to be submitted by each partner are:

- application of the feasibility report for examination and approval
- project proposal and approval documents
- feasibility study report
- certificate of legal representatives of each of the contracting parties
- banks and other financial statements or references for each of the contracting party
- comments on environmental and fire protection, labor safety, sanitation, etc by the various authorities
- evaluation report and comments on the feasibility report by the relevant authorities

Examination and Approval of Contract and Articles of Association

Each party to the contract must submit the following documents to MOFTEC or its authorized representative for approval:

- project proposal and approval document
- feasibility study report and approval document
- contract and articles of association signed by the parties involved
- copy of business license and registration
- bank references of foreign investor(s)
- names of Board of Directors and documents on appointment
- registration of name

Once the contract and articles of association are approved, an application for the approval certificate for establishing an enterprise with foreign investment is required. For this, the documents required are:

- application form for enterprises with foreign investment

- business license, registration certificate and bank reference of foreign party(s)
- business license of the Chinese party
- project proposal, feasibility study report and approval document
- contract, articles of association and approval document
- name of directors, chairman, general manager and document of appointment
- registration of name of company

Registration with Statistics Department

Upon receipt of the approval certificate, registration with the statistics department is required. Take along these documents:
- original copy of approval certificate of the enterprise
- statistics registration form, completed in duplicate, for the enterprise

Registration with the Administration for Industry and Commerce

This must be done within 30 days after receiving approval for all of the above. Documents required for this application are:
- four copies of the application signed by the Chairman and Vice Chairman of the enterprise
- contract and articles of association in Chinese or Chinese and a foreign language, and two copies of approval documents and certificates
- project proposal, feasibility study report and approval documents
- business license of the foreign party
- bank reference of the foreign party
- list of names of directors, chairman, vice chairman and general manager

Registration of Land Use Rights

Certain ventures with foreign investment (for example, real estate investments) must apply to the land administration department for rights to land use.

Registration with Administration of Foreign Exchange Control
Within 15 days of getting the business license, the enterprise must register with the State Administration of Foreign Exchange Control with the following documents.

- copy of business license issued by the Administration for Industry and Commerce.
- copy of approval certificate for the establishment of the enterprise
- copy of contract and articles of association

Opening a Bank Account
To open a foreign and/or RMB currency account, the following documents are required:

- business license issued by the Administration of Industry and Commerce
- certificate of approval for establishment of the enterprise

Registration for Taxation
Within 30 days from receiving the business license, an enterprise must register with the relevant taxation department.

The documents required for this are.

- copy of business license issued by the Administration of Industry and Commerce.
- contract and articles of association and approval document
- approval certificate for establishment of the enterprise
- feasibility study report and approval document
- list of names of the Board of Directors

Registration with the Customs Department
Documents required for registration are:

- approval certificate for establishment of enterprise
- business license
- contract and articles of association
- inventory of approved import equipment
- report of verification of capital

Documents for registration of declaration:
- approval certificate for establishment of enterprise
- business license
- official written reply from the Commission of Economic Relation and Trade

Documents for examination and approval of exemption from customs duties:
- certificate of exemption from taxes for imported goods
- invoices
- copy of the permit
- customs debenture of imported or exported goods
- packing list
- bill of lading

Registration with the Finance Administration
Finally, the enterprise must register with the Finance Administration authority.
Documents required are:
- copy of business license
- certificate of approval for establishment of enterprise
- feasibility study report and approval document
- contract and articles of association

Registered Capital and Total Investment
Legislation set by the Administration of Industry and Commerce on rate of registered capital to total investment of enterprises with foreign investments is as follows:

Total Investment in (US$)	Rate of Registered Capital to Total Investment
Below 3 million	7:10
3 million to 10 million	1:2
10 million to 30 million	2:5
30 million and above	1:3

If your total investment is US$10 million, your paid-up capital must be at least 50% of this sum, or US$5 million.

Limits of Approving Authorities for Mega Projects

Foreign investment projects must be in line with China's industrial development policies. Proposals are submitted to the respective departments of the State, the Beijing municipality, or district/county government, according to the size and type of investment.

Proposals for mega projects and Sino-foreign joint ventures or joint co-operatives with investments in excess of US$100 million are submitted to the State Planning Commission and approved by the State Council.

For joint ventures or joint co-operatives with investments of between US$30 million and US$100 million, project proposals and feasibility reports are submitted to the Beijing (provincial or municipal) Planning Commission and approved by the State Planning Commission.

Project proposals and feasibility reports for joint ventures or joint co-operatives with investments of between US$5 million and US$30 million for the first and second industries and over US$3 million for the tertiary industry are submitted to the Beijing Planning Commission for approval.

Project proposals, feasibility reports, Contracts and Articles of Association for joint ventures or joint co-operatives with investments of less than US$5 million in the first and second industries or with less than US$3 million in the tertiary industry are submitted to the districts or counties for approval.

For joint ventures or co-operatives set up in Beijing's Economic and Technological Development Zones involving investments of less than US$30 million in the industrial sector, or investments of less than US$3 million in the tertiary industry, the project proposals and feasibility reports are submitted to the Development Zone administration for verification and approval. The Contracts and Articles of Association for such ventures with investments of less than US$10 million are submitted to and approved by the Development Zone administration.

Do remember though that the local officials do not always adhere to such limits, particularly if the local government or the entity directly under its control has a joint venture agreement with you. Very often, projects are divided into phases or even under-declared so that it is within their approving limit instead of at state or provincial level. Approval at local levels is faster and much more convenient. A word of caution: the State Planning Commission can nullify it if the inconsistency is found.

Agreements and Contracts

The Chinese prefer a simple agreement and/or contract. However, like their laws and regulations, over-simplification can lead to ambiguity in interpretation and create unnecessary complications. Foreign business people who request more details are often told that the small details are "small problems which can be resolved later, as, after all, we will soon be one family." If you succumb to this line of reasoning, you will have cause to regret it later.

At the same time, avoid going to the other extreme. The Chinese take offence if every word in the agreement and/or contract is screened and amended. As all agreements and contracts are in Chinese, and the Chinese version takes precedence over other translations, it may not be worth your while arguing over theoretical and/or hypothetical issues in the interpretation of your draft.

Be practical but make sure that the agreement and contract cover all major issues so that there will be a basis for resolution in the event of a dispute.

Joint Ventures

Under Chinese legislation, participants in a joint venture shall be "the legal person of the enterprises." A legal person of an enterprise and/or other economic organization is one having the legal qualification acquired in accordance with Clauses 36 to 39 of the

"General Rules of Civil Law." It includes state-owned, collective or private enterprises.

Private individuals and others not having the legal qualification are not allowed to establish a joint venture enterprise with foreigners. Under Chinese corporate laws, the individual has no legal standing other than as a representative of a duly constituted company or group of companies. Partnerships and sole proprietorships, which are common in other countries, are non-existent and not recognized in China.

A Sino-foreign joint venture enterprise incorporated in China is governed by the laws of China and hence considered a Chinese entity in the eyes of the law. Unlike foreigners, a Sino-foreign joint venture enterprise can purchase properties meant for the locals. They can buy up-market local apartments instead of those meant for foreigners, and developers are changing their emphasis to focus on this sector of the property market since the development cost is very much lower and the profit margin higher.

Sino-foreign joint ventures can also engage in real estate development in China. For this, it has to find a local partner(s) who owns a real estate development license, since new licenses are difficult to get.

The Board of Directors   Under the joint venture law of China, the Board of Directors must comprise no fewer than three Directors. The shareholders shall decide the allocation and appointment of directors, chairman and vice chairman. In general, the number of directors from each party is proportionate to their shares in the joint venture. If the foreign party takes the post of chairman, the vice-chairmanship will normally go to the Chinese party and vice versa. The same applies to the appointment of the general manager and the deputy general manager. The term of office is normally four or five years and may be extended if so decided by the Board of Directors. The chairman is the legal representative of the joint venture company.

The Board of Directors Meeting It is a requirement that the Board of Directors must meet at least once every year. The Board of Directors meeting shall be presided over by the chairman. If he is not available, the vice-chairman or a director presides. Apart from the annual meeting, the Board of Directors may convene a meeting if proposed by at least one third of the members. Two-thirds of the members are required to form a quorum for these meetings. Proxies are allowed but this has to done in writing.

A simple majority is required for most issues brought before the Board of Directors except the following, which require unanimous agreement from all members:

- amendment to the articles of association
- suspension and/or dissolution of the joint venture
- increase in or assignment of registered capital
- merger of any kind.

The General Manager State-owned enterprises do not normally have a managing director. The general manager is the boss of the company and the legal representative of the company.

In a joint venture company in China, the general manager is the most important individual in the company. He is responsible for carrying out the Board of Directors' decisions and for organizing and conducting the day-to-day operations of the company. Depending on the agreement in the Articles of Association of the joint venture, the general manager is normally empowered to carry out all matters on behalf of the Board of Directors. Certain major issues may require the consensus of his deputies.

The general manager and his deputies may concurrently be members of the Board of Directors. They are, however, prohibited by law from holding similar positions in other enterprises for fear of a conflict of interest. However, most investors choose to ignore this ruling and it is quite common to find a person holding several positions in various companies.

Representative Office

The setting up of a representative office of a foreign enterprise in China will only be approved if its scope of operation does not involve any direct profit-making activities. A representative office can only perform activities such as data collection, establishing business contacts or connections, product introduction or marketing, technology exchange, etc. which does not generate direct income.

In applying for the establishment of a representative office in China, the foreign enterprise must first have a guarantor who must be a Chinese organization acceptable to the authority. The guarantor who sponsors the formation of the representative office is officially responsible for the foreign enterprise. Applications are submitted to MOFTEC. To facilitate this, the Foreign Investment Service Centre (FISC) is authorized by MOFTEC to accept a commission from the foreign enterprises to handle the application and approving processes.

Procedures and Documents

- Documents giving the background of the enterprise, scope of business, purpose of setting up the office, location and operational terms etc. must be submitted with the application which must be signed by the Chairman or President together with the official seal of the enterprise.
- Letter of attorney or certificate of authorization by the Chairman or President for the representative(s) to act for the enterprise.
- Business license of the enterprise
- Bank statements and financial references.
- Resume of the representative(s) together with identification (passport) and two photographs of each representative.
- A letter of appointment with the FISC, signed by the enterprise, to handle the various processes until the certificate of approval is received.

Normally, the authorities will examine and approve (or reject) the application within 30 days from the date of receipt of the application. When the application is approved, the authority will issue a certificate of registration after a registration fee is paid.

Upon approval, the representative office of the foreign enterprise must register with the Public Security Bureau, the banks and the customs and tax authorities and other departments for residence permits and other related matters. The representative office is deemed to be officially established from the date of its registration. Thereafter, its activities in China are governed and protected by the laws of the People's Republic of China.

The registration certificate is only valid for a period of one year, and can be renewed 30 days before expiry. To renew, an annual report (in Chinese) of its business operations must be submitted with the application for renewal.

A change of name of the office, or the number of representatives and their names, or the scope of the business, or the address of the resident office must be filed with the registration office. A change of representatives requires a power of attorney from the foreign enterprise together with the resumes of the new representatives.

If bankruptcy or premature termination of its business operations is declared, it must go through the deregistration procedures at the registration office and produce documents issued by the tax authorities, banks and customs to certify the cleaning up of taxes, debts and other related matters before approval is granted. For any unsettled matters, the foreign enterprise, its representatives and the guarantor are held responsible.

MOFTEC and the Administrations for Industry & Commerce in the provinces, municipalities and other autonomous regions are empowered to supervise and inspect the business activities of the representative office within their jurisdiction. The representative office is required to co-operate and provide all necessary information and material as required.

The following violations are punishable by the State Administration for Industry and Commerce according to the seriousness of the case:

- If the resident office of a foreign enterprise is proven to have engaged in direct profit-making operations in violation of the conditions for its registration, it will be ordered to stop its business operations and made to pay a fine of not exceeding RMB20,000.

- If the resident office of a foreign enterprise is proven to have altered any item in the register without going through the required procedures or fail to de-register when it should have, it will be given a notice of warning. For more serious cases, a fine not exceeding RMB5,000/- shall be imposed or the registration certificate may even be revoked.

- When the resident office of a foreign enterprise is found to have engaged in speculation, swindling and other unlawful activities, all proceeds and properties thus obtained will be confiscated in addition to a fine or even the cancellation of the registration certificate as the case may be. Cases that violate the criminal code of PRC shall be brought before the court and punished according to that law.

Real Estate Development

Real estate property development is the most popular form of investment among the overseas Chinese in China because of the relatively quick returns on investment.

The procedures for setting up a real estate development company are basically the same as with other companies but you will need to acquire the Land Use Rights for the development site.

This is also the industry singled out as one of the main causes of excessive inflation in the Chinese economy because of the huge volume of activities in this sector. To engage in such a venture, it is necessary to find a local partner(s) who owns a real estate development license, since new licenses are difficult to get. Real estate developers are also classified into a few categories according to their size and experience. Restrictions are also set for the various categories to limit their activities accordingly. Therefore it is necessary to find a partner with the appropriate license.

Import and Export Businesses

Companies dealing exclusively in import and export businesses are not allowed. There are however a few exceptions approved by the Central Government.

Imports are closely monitored by the State Government and are carried out exclusively by government agencies. Except for a few controlled items, the Chinese Government encourages and in fact provides various incentives for the export of local products. Foreign enterprises involved in manufacturing in China can, and are encouraged to, export their manufactured products. Foreign enterprises and Sino-foreign joint venture enterprises engaged in the production of goods for local consumption are even encouraged to export local products (other than their own) for foreign exchange.

Retailing

Retail business licenses are very tightly controlled by the State Government and only a handful of such licenses are known to have been officially issued to Sino-foreign joint ventures.

Although there are large numbers of Sino-foreign-owned retail stores in China, particularly in Shanghai and Beijing, most of these stores operate by *bian tong bang fa* or what the Chinese call "working around the system". Since getting a retail license is a problem, most of these companies operate using their local partner's license.

Window display in a high-end shop

Example 1
ABC Departmental Store Ltd forms a joint venture AZ Retail Ltd with XYZ Departmental Store of China. XYZ has a retail license. So, AZ Retail Ltd will have to sign a separate agreement with XYZ to use their license for operation.

Example 2
A joint venture company is formed between a giant Japanese retail chain and a large departmental store in China to build a large shopping complex. The complex is then divided into two halves (provided for at the design stage) according to their prior agreement and share proportion. Both parties then operate their stores within this building, independent of each other. However, as the Japanese retail store has to operate under the license of the local partner, it pays a fee based on its turnover to the local partner.

Example 3
AZ Retail Ltd (as in the first example) leases and operates half the retail space within XYZ Departmental Store's shopping complex. AZ Retail Ltd can operate this store as if it is a separate entity, but it must be operated under XYZ Departmental Store's license.

Officially, for taxes, accounting and even issuing of receipts, these entities make use of their local partners.

Branch Offices
Branch offices will have to go through the same approving process as a new company. All documents, including those of their main operations in China, will have to be submitted to the Industrial and Commercial Administration Department where the branches are to be established.

CHAPTER 14

Learning Experiences

Here are some true-life incidents to illustrate the culture, expectations, and mindset of people you will deal with when venturing into China.

Perpetual Entertainment at the State's Expense

After two weeks in Shanghai, I noticed the same people dining at the restaurant of the hotel where I was staying in. Out of curiosity, I asked the restaurant manager.

Shaking his head, the restaurant manager explained that most of them were senior managers in state-owned organizations in that district. They each took turns to entertain one another all year round at this expensive restaurant, at State expense. Also, the restaurant actually gives them a receipt for a much higher value than what they spent. Therefore, when they make a claim for reimbursement, they also get additional money on the side.

Staying Away from Work

Most state-owned enterprises are grossly overstaffed because of the policy of job allocation adopted by the State government. Having too much time in hand, employees co-operate to stay away from work.

A typical example was this young Chinese friend of mine called Xiao Wang. Whenever I was in Beijing, he was always around to keep me company, no matter how long I stayed. One day when I told him not to waste his annual leave, he laughed and told me that he was not on leave. He assured me that as far as his factory was concerned, he was working. He then picked up the telephone, dialed his office number and handed me the phone. "Ask for me," he said. I did, and was told by the person at the other end that this young friend of mine "had just stepped out of the office five minutes ago."

Xiao Wang then explained that whenever he wanted to stay away from work, he would inform his colleague who would switch on Xiao Wang's table lamp and insert the key to his desk. In the evening, at about 4:30 p.m., the key would be removed and the lights switched off. If there was a telephone call for Xiao Wang, the caller would be told that he had just stepped out of the office. Apparently, not even the manager is concerned about his absence.

He also assured me that there were thousands of workers each day who go on 'long' medical leave with purchased medical certificates.

Driving within the Rules of Law but without a License

A friend of mine arrived in Shanghai without his Chinese driving license. As he needed to drive some guests around for a day or two, he turned to my driver, who had a friend in the traffic police department, for help. With a carton of imported cigarettes, my friend received a temporary license.

First, the police issued him a "ticket" stating that his driving license had been compounded and held in the traffic police department. The "ticket" allowed him to drive for three days from the date the license was confiscated.

Bu pa guan, zi pa kuan

This simply means not to fear the officer (the one at the top) but the people at the bottom who supervise your work. All too often, the foreign investor underestimates the influence they have and the problems they can cause.

Example

The Chairman of a big conglomerate wanted to build a mega-complex on the busiest street in Beijing. Through the local network, he got in touch with the Vice-Mayor responsible for the city development. The Mayor then arranged for a few pieces of land for him to select. At a special dinner meeting with the local officials, the Vice-Mayor instructed the District Officer in Charge, to finalize the details for the sale of the land to the investor. He also instructed the local officials to ensure "green light" (*kai lu deng*) or, in other words, clear the path for the application and to assist the investor and ensure smooth progress for the project.

After the briefing from the Vice-Mayor, the District Officer was left to negotiate with the investor's resident director. The discussions were very cordial, but beneath the smiles, the resident director felt a strong resentment among the Chinese party.

During the negotiations, he encountered obstacles—the price quoted shot up to US$850 per sq m from US$750 per sq m and certain restrictive conditions were imposed.

In trying to resolve the situation, the Chairman made an interesting find. Apparently, in seeking the Vice-Mayor's help for the land, he had greatly upset the District Officer. According to a local associate, that piece of land was a "gold mine" for the local officers. The norm was to have such land given out in the form of direct sales or for joint ventures with foreigners. Middlemen are then hired who will demand agency fees and other administrative costs from the foreign investors. This goes into the pockets of the local officials.

As the investor had requested the land through the Vice-Mayor, the local officers' hopes for commissions and extras were dashed. They were very upset but yet could not appear to be difficult or not co-operative, as that would mean not 'giving face' to the Vice-Mayor.

Realizing the problems, the investor then sent a local associate to visit the District Officer privately to resolve the situation for the benefit of all concerned. The District Officer was very happy; he immediately suggested that the investor talk to his agent who was then handling another project, which they were trying to sell and/or get a joint venture partner for.

This other project involved a half-completed office and commercial complex at one of the busiest MRT stations in downtown Beijing. It was actually a much better project. The final negotiation took a day and the investor was able to close the deal at a much lower cost. Everyone was appeased as a commission was paid to the "agent" for the deal.

Ren zi bu shi fa zi

This phrase simply means that China is ruled by the people and not by the law, that is, laws can be interpreted to suit local interest. It is a difficult rule for many foreigners to understand.

Individual Interest takes Precedence over that of the State

It was the opening day of a grand discount promotion in a new department store of our subsidiary company in Wuhan. I was touring the store with our divisional General Manager responsible for retail. The store was crowded because of the much-publicized promotion. However, when we passed the Office Equipment Department, there was a very distinct quietness although big discount signs were posted prominently everywhere as in all the other sections in the store. The General Manager was rather disappointed and went round checking the displays, price tags and discount signs.

Back in his office, I asked him who would be his main customers for the office equipment. "Offices in and around this area I guess," he replied. "Fine, and if that is the case, I would imagine that most of them would be state-owned enterprises, right?" I asked. I told him that the discount would not make any difference to his sales because government officials could not care less if the piece of equipment cost only half the price. "Try replacing the discounts with free gifts", I suggested.

The discounts for office equipment were then replaced with free gifts ranging from fanciful toys to mini-radios and Walkmans. The sales immediately doubled. The free gifts were more important to the purchasers than the items that they purchased as the officials kept the free gifts for themselves.

We learnt an important lesson—that personal gains take priority over official matters.

Unusual Behavior In Hotels
Those involved in the hotel business will note certain peculiarities:

i) Damage from cigarettes
As most Chinese smoke, common scenes in hotel rooms are burnt carpets (it is a habit among the locals to throw cigarette butts onto the floor as most homes and offices have cement floor) and burnt sheets or blankets.

ii) Disappearing items
Toiletries, towels, ashtrays, robes and even paintings have been known to disappear from hotel rooms. These are proudly displayed in their homes as a souvenir of their stay in such hotels.

iii) Emptying the mini-bars
There is also the practise of emptying the mini-bar or fridge in their hotel rooms even though they are fully aware that the drinks and snacks are cheaper outside the hotel. The reasons are simple: items removed from the hotel are charged to the hotel bill which is paid by the company or the State Government.

Conclusion and final word of advice
China's economic reform and the "open door policy" adopted since late 1978 has been a great success. From the city of Shanghai to the autonomous region in Tibet, everyone has benefited from the reforms and the economic boom in varying degrees. However,

while China is inundated with foreign investors, not all foreign investors have been successful. A good place to exchange notes and learn from one another's experiences is at functions and gatherings of foreign investors. It cannot be emphasized enough that success in business in China comes with adjustment of one's mentality and expectations first, and an understanding of the culture, mindset and business environment of the people and the country.

Basic Facts & Travel Tips

Climate

China has a land mass of 9,600,000 square kilometers, with borders along the Mongolian People's Republic in the north, to North Korea in the northeast and Vietnam, Laos, Myanmar, India and Pakistan in the west and northwest.

Its climate therefore ranges from the severe cold of Siberia up north, to a sub-tropical climate in the south. In winter, the temperature in cities like Heilongjiang can dip close to −40°C, while places like Wuhan can be a steaming 45°C in summer. Generally, the northern part of China has cold, dry winters and hot summers with periodic droughts when the monsoon rains are delayed or missed. South China has ample rainfall and a relatively higher temperature.

For conservation purposes, and also because of a shortage of resources, it was decreed some decades ago, that the Yangtse River would be the demarcation for areas that need heating in winter. Because of this ruling, you will find that offices and homes up north of the Yangtse River are nice and warm in winter while those in the south are miserably cold. This still applies to State-owned offices and local homes.

Travel

You can get to China by air, sea or land. However, because of the vast differences in the stage of development of the many provinces and cities, airport conditions vary from the worst of the third world to the best of international ones.

Major cities like Beijing, Shanghai and Shenzhen are well served by local and international airlines. You can catch a flight out of the country from these cities to most major cities in the world. International flights from other cities in China are still quite limited and infrequent as most flights to these cities are normally via Beijing, Shanghai, Shenzhen and Hong Kong.

Domestic airlines provide flights for inland travel to most parts of China but they are limited and crowded. Flights between or to some of the smaller cities may only be available once or twice a week. Travelers are therefore advised to book their flight well in advance, or they may find themselves in these small cities for longer than they wish.

A trip on a domestic flight can be quite an experience. For smaller planes, there is only one class of seats and it is normally full. Overbooking is common. Computer failure was common in the earlier days and passengers joining flights from another city could be given boarding passes without a seat allocation. In such a situation, you would find them pushing and elbowing their way up the plane to ensure that they get the best seats.

In China, the Chinese do not believe in checking-in their luggage. Carrying huge canvas bags on their backs and a few more pieces of hand luggage in both hands up the plane is common. You may also find, as part of their hand luggage, livestock which they are taking as a gift to a friend or relative they are visiting. Normally there will not be enough space in the overhead luggage compartments on the plane and the extra luggage ends up crowding the aisle, so much so that one has to climb over them to get to one's seat.

Travel by sea to China is limited to cities in the south like Guangzhou and Shenzhen from Hong Kong. Trains from Hong Kong to Guangzhou and Shenzhen are also very convenient. It is also possible to get into China by rail from Europe via Russia.

Traveling within China by rail can be quite an experience. Basically there are two classes of train travel within China. The economy or "hard seat" compartments are meant for the local people while the luxury class or "soft seat" compartments are meant for senior officials and foreigners.

Visas

Visas are required for practically all foreigners visiting China, whether as a tourist or on business. These are issued by the Chinese embassy or consulate in the respective country of the traveler. Travelers from countries that do not have diplomatic ties with China will have to apply for their visa through another country with diplomatic ties or Hong Kong. For short visits, visas may be obtained on the spot from the immigration counters at the ports, airports or train stations in major cities like Beijing, Shanghai and Shenzhen. Normally the visa is good for a visit of less than a week with the possibility of an extension if necessary.

Health

Health declaration is required by immigration when you visit the country. Visitors from known infected areas are required to show proof of inoculation against diseases like cholera and yellow fever. Long-term residents and those on business in China are required to show proof that they are not infected with AIDs.

China has many well-trained western-styled medical practitioners as well as traditional medical practitioners. Unfortunately, the equipment they use are often old and obsolete.

Most Chinese prefer traditional Chinese medication to western drugs because of the belief that the natural herbs produce less side effects.

There are now many private hospitals run by Sino-foreign joint ventures in cities like Beijing and Shanghai where facilities are comparable with those in the developed countries. Foreign-trained doctors are usually found in such hospitals.

Frequent travelers to China are advised to have their vaccinations against hepatitis A and B before they arrive in China. It is not safe to drink off the tap. Always drink bottled or boiled water. When patronizing roadside stalls, choose piping hot food.

A food stall by the road

Keeping fit

Most Chinese keep fit through cycling which is their main means of transport, irrespective of age. On mornings and weekends, you will find gardens, parks, sidewalks and all other available open space packed with people doing tai chi, kung fu, or aerobic dances. In the early evenings, these places are venues for open-air disco and ballroom dancing, and tai chi practise. Jogging is not as popular among the Chinese. There are limited gyms for the general public and they are mainly in good class hotels and condos and therefore limited to the foreigners and young professionals.

Getting around town

There is no problem getting around in big cities in China but in remote areas such as Guiyang, this can be quite troublesome.

Mass rail transit or subway systems are only available in big cities like Beijing, Shanghai, Guangzhou and Tianjin. The system in Beijing was first built in the 1960s and is therefore very old but it still serves as the main means of transport within the city. Shanghai has a relatively new subway system, comparable to the best in developed countries. The routes in all these cities are, however, very limited. Notwithstanding this, the subway system greatly helps in reducing the traffic congestion caused by bicycles.

Buses are the most common form of transport. These are normally electric trams and cover most parts of the cities. The fares are very cheap as the government heavily subsidizes them. There will normally be a driver and a conductor on the buses or trams. The conductor sells and issues tickets, and yells out the various stops.

Taxis are probably the best way to get around for most foreigners. Before the mid-80s, taxis were operated by state-owned enterprises and the fares were fairer. Privately owned taxis have now begun to make their appearance. Make sure that the meter is switched on to avoid arguments over exorbitant charges.

If you feel that you have been overcharged, insist on a receipt. Record the time of travel and the vehicle registration number on the receipt. Usually at this point, the driver will offer a discount to stop you from making a complaint to the authority, as they may lose their license.

Bigger cars like the Toyota Crown and Nissan Cedric charge a higher tariff and are normally for tourists. Mini-vans are popular among the locals and they charge a much lower fare.

Because of the amount of cash they carry in the taxis, taxi drivers are the subject of many robberies. To protect them, there is even a ruling in some cities that taxi drivers should have a companion when operating after 8:00 p.m.

Tricycles are vehicles that consist of a two-seater cabin attached to either a bicycle or a motorcycle. In the suburbs, these are the common means of transportation along the main bus routes.

Bicycles are the most common means of transportation among the locals. Almost every Chinese rides one. In Beijing and Shanghai, the number of bicycles almost equals the population.

Food

Chinese cuisine is well-known for its excellent taste and variety.

Most restaurants in China are noisy and smoke-filled but certain restaurants have a separate section for foreigners. These are generally cleaner.

Chinese cuisine can be classified under four broad categories based on the regions:

Southern cuisine includes food of the southern region, and of Canton, Fujian and Taiwan. Even among them, there are differences in terms of flavor and cooking styles. Southern cuisine uses more seafood because of the region's proximity to the sea. The emphasis is on retaining the natural flavors of the food, and strong spices are seldom used. Rice is normally served with the food.

Eastern cuisine from Shanghai, Jiangsu, Zhejiang and the surrounding areas uses lots of beef, pork, chicken and vegetables. The food tends to be saltier and oily. Vinegar is often used in many of the dishes. Rice is usually served with the food.

Northern cuisine from the northern region of Hebei (Beijing), Henan, Shangdong, Shanxi uses beef, lamb and duck. Like the eastern cuisine, the food is quite salty and oily. The northerners consume plenty of garlic and vinegar. Buns are preferred to rice.

Western cuisine from the Sichuan and Hunan provinces is famous for its fiery hot pepper and tongue-numbing spices. Food also tends to be quite salty in these regions. Like the northerners, they prefer buns to rice.

Cost of living

The cost of living for the local people in China is relatively low by international standards as there are heavy government subsidies for housing, utilities, transport, medical needs, education and certain basic necessities.

Foreigners find housing costs in Beijing and Shanghai among the most expensive in the world.

Dressing

Before the mid-1980s, the only colors seen in Chinese clothes were green, blue and grey in the uniforms of the armed forces and/or Mao's jackets issued by the *danwei*. Bright colors like yellow and red were exclusively for children. Now, Shanghai, Guangzhou, Beijing and even Chengdu are getting more fashionable than Hong Kong.

Winter finds the Chinese wrapped up in thick clothing and leather jackets.

Summer in the south can be unbearably hot when temperature averages between 35°C to 42°C. Light, thin and often transparent short-sleeved shirts and sandals become popular with the men and you may even find them rolling up their trousers to their knees. This is also when young ladies take to hot-pants, mini skirts and tank-tops.

There are no hard and fast rules as to how foreigners should dress but a jacket and tie for men is considered formal for a function. Ladies should avoid clothing which are too revealing.

Accommodation

Fairly reasonable accommodation is available in major cities like Shanghai and Beijing but prices are high both for sale and rent. Some foreigners resort to staying in local apartments in these cities. This is illegal as foreigners are not allowed to stay in local apartments.

As a rule, the local Public Security Bureau keeps fairly detailed records of all the local residents within their districts. Foreigners are kept out of this, as a different monitoring system for foreigners applies. It is thus not advisable for foreigners to stay in apartments for local residents, especially in the smaller cities where their presence is quite obvious.

Serviced apartments and hotels are available for foreigners as well as non-rated local hotels and guesthouses. In the local hotels and guesthouses, you will find a service counter at each floor where the attendants, apart from attending to your needs, also keep records of your movements in and out of the room.

There are basically five categories of hotels and accommodation:

1) *Zhao dai suo* meaning "reception area or room."

These are for the local traveler. Facilities are very basic with four to sixteen beds in each room, dormitory-style. Some may have VIP rooms with one or two beds per room. Bathrooms and toilets are shared by all guests. In cities located south of the Yangtse River, hot water may not be available in the baths or showers even in winter.

2) *Lu guan* meaning a place catering to tours.

These are hotels meant for the local tourist and facilities are slightly better than those found in the *zhao dai suo*. There may be one to four beds in each room. Toilets and bathing facilities are shared.

3) *Bin guan* meaning a place for guests.

These are local hotels with less than three-star rating. Again furnishing is very basic. When I stayed in one of them in the late 1980s, hotel guests were not given the keys to their rooms. Instead, the keys were kept by the housekeepers at the service counter at each floor and you need to inform the housekeeper each time you go to your room.

4) *Jiu dian* meaning liquor shop or store.
These are the bigger hotels, irrespective of grading.

5) *Fan dian* meaning a rice shop or a place for meals.
Again, these mean the big hotels.

Shopping

There is a huge variety of goods available in China, ranging from the cheapest to the most expensive. As in most countries, tour guides often receive a commission for bringing in customers.

Most mega-stores are state-owned. The smaller stores are mostly private enterprises or foreign joint ventures. Foreign-run departmental stores and supermarket chains like Isetan and Parkson are very popular among the locals. You can find branded stores like Dunhill and Gucci in the upmarket areas and five-star international hotels.

Garments. In Beijing, shops along Xi'dan Road offer some of the best deals for garments and is very popular with the local shoppers. Xiu Shiu Lu is a popular wholesale center for garments, especially silk garments. You will find large groups of Russians buying the garments for export back to Russia. If you are shopping in this area, do not be afraid to bargain. Bargaining is expected and you can counter offer at even half the price.

In Shanghai, Nanjing Lu is popular among local as well as international tourists. Often, local visitors buy and resell the goods in their villages. Goods from Shanghai are reputed to be classier and more up-to-date and therefore more expensive. Nanjing Lu is a 'must see' in Shanghai because of its history and, apparently, if you have not been to Nanjing Lu, you cannot claim to have been to Shanghai.

Huai Hai Lu is another popular shopping haunt. It caters to trendy locals and foreigners who are resident in Shanghai.

Antiques and paintings. Unless you are an expert in this area, it is advisable to purchase such items from state-owned and other reputable shops because there are many imitations. State-owned enterprises and universities sell reproductions as souvenirs to tourists. Many are as good as the original and you will be specifically informed that they are imitations.

Keep away from people claiming that they have a stolen national treasure for sale to you cheaply. Even if they are genuine, remember that if you are caught in possession of a national treasure, you will be in real trouble.

Safety and the law

Generally it is safe to venture out even in the night as long as you stay away from isolated places. Most cities in China are peaceful and enjoy a very low crime rate. The police are efficient and the laws stringent. Punishment is stiff and swift. The penalty for armed robberies and rapes is death.

Common Phrases

Ai ren （爱人）Spouse, husband or wife in China. Outside China, this simply means lover or sweetheart.

Ban shi yao kan qian hou（办事要看前后）This means that you have to consider all possiblities and consequences when doing something.

Ban shi yao kan qian hou （办事要看钱厚）With the last two words changed but having the same pronunciation, this expression means that action will be taken depending on the thickness (amount) of money.

Bao fu（包袱）This literally means burden and refers to invalids and retirees in state-owned enterprises.

Bai hua dong（百花动）The hundred flowers movement in which intellectuals were encouraged to voice their political opinions followed by Anti-Rightist Campaign in which dissenters were purged.

Bian tong ban fa（变通办法）This means a modified or alternative method.

Bin guan(宾馆) Small hotel.

Bu pa guan, zhi pa guan (不怕官，只怕管) Worry not about the officer but the person directly responsible, that is, do not worry about the boss but be wary of the guy supervising your job.

Bu gei mian zi(不给面子) Not giving face.

Cheng bao(承包) Sub-contracting system.

Cheng shang ming biao(程上名表) To submit a name list.

Cheng shang ming biao(程上名表) The other meaning is to submit a branded watch.

Da zuo, da cuo(大做大错)

Xiao zuo xiao cuo(小做小错)

Bu zuo bu cuo(不做不错) The more you work, the greater your chances of making mistakes. The less you work, the less your chances of making mistakes. If you do not work, there will be no opportunity for you to make a mistake.

Dangan(档案) A personal file of the history of each Chinese citizen.

Danwei (单位) Work unit or organization.

Diu lian(丢脸) To lose face.

Diao yu(钓鱼) Fishing, or to hook someone.

Fan dian (饭店) Hotel.

Gao guan xi (搞关系) Make or establish a connection.

Ge ti hu (个体户) Private enterprise.

Guan xi (关系) Connection or relationship.

Guan xi wang(关系网) Connection network.

Hong wei bing(红卫兵) The red guards during the Cultural Revolution.

Hongben(红本) Chinese equivalent of a land title.

Houmen(后门) Backdoor.

Hua bo tu di(划拨土地) Rights of use through assignment or grant.

Hun(混) To be idle or float along.

Jian ji xing shi(见机行事) To act according to circumstances or situation but the other meaning is, action will be taken after receipt of a TV set.

Jing mao bu (经贸部) Department for Trade and Commerce.

Jiu dian (酒店) Hotel.

La guan xi (拉关系) Pulling strings.

Li run liu cheng (利润流程) Profit Retention Scheme.

Lu guan (旅馆) Small hotel.

Mian zi (面子) Face or a person's self respect.

Nan (男) Male.

Nan or *nu peng you* (男 / 女朋友) Male/female friend but in China it means lover or sweetheart.

Nu (女) Female.

Peng you (朋友) Friend.

Pi zu (批租) Acquisition of land by out-right lease/ transfer.

Ren duo hao ban shi (人多好办事) Easier to get work done with more people. Mao's ideology to encourage childbirth.

Ren zhi bu shi fa zhi (人制，不是法制) Ruled by the people and not by the law.

Shan gao huang di yuan (山高皇帝远) The mountain is high and the Emperor is far away, meaning that it is beyond the control of the authorities.

Shang you zheng ce, xia you dui ce (上有政策，下有对策) The top may have a policy (or regulation or law), below we have a counter policy.

Si ren bang (四人帮) The infamous Gang of Four who manipulated the aging Mao during the last few years before his death.

Sun zi bing fa (孙子兵法) The well-known *Sunzi Art of War.*

Tiao jie shui (调解税) Adjustment tax.

Tie fan wan (铁饭碗) Iron rice bowl.

Tong zhi (同志) Comrade.

Xia hai (下海) Taking a plunge into the sea, which means throwing away the iron rice bowl to join the private sector.

Xiang cun qi ye (乡村企业) Village enterprise.

Yan jiu (研究) To discuss, deliberate or explore.

Yan jiu (烟酒) Cigarettes and wine.

Zhao dai suo (招待所) Local guest house.

Zhi ji zhi bi, bai zhan bai sheng (知己知彼，百战百胜) Know yourself, know your enemies, a hundred battles, a hundred victories—A famous ideology in Sunzi's *Art of War*.

Gao yuan zi dan bu ru mai cha ye dan (搞原子弹，不如卖茶叶蛋) The person doing research and development on atomic bombs cannot be compared with the person selling eggs cooked in tea leaves and soya source. (Bombs and eggs sound the same in Chinese or *Putong Hua*)

Na shou shu dao bu ru na zhu rou dao (拿手术刀，不如拿猪肉刀) The person using the surgical knife (the surgeon) cannot be compared with the person holding the butcher's knife.

Bu gei mian zi or bu gei lian (不给面子) Not giving face.

Diu lian (丢脸) To lose face.

Wen ti bu da (问题不大) Problem not big—this expression normally implies there there is no problem—but can be turned around to mean that there were problems, although not big.

Xiao wen ti (小问题) Small problem—same meaning as *wenti bu da*.

Tong gong tong chou (同工同酬) Same work, same pay.

Jing di zhi wa (井底之蛙) A frog in the well.

Fa ren dai biao (法人代表) A legal representative.

Directory of Important Contacts

**Ministry of Foreign Trade &
Economic Co-operation**
2 Dongchangan Jie, Beijing
100730.
www.moftec.gov.cn
Tel: 86-10-6519 8114

**State Economic & Trade
Commission**
26 Xuanwumen Xi Jie, Beijing
10005334-35
Tel: 86-10-6394 5531

**State Administration of
Import / Export Commodity
Inspection**
15 Fangcaodi Xi Jie, Beijing
100020
Tel: 86-10-6500 7744

**Civil Aviation Administration
of China**
155 Dongsi Da Jie, Beijing
100710
Tel: 86-10-6401 2233

Ministry of Finance
Sanlihe, Xichengqu, Beijing
100820
www.mof.gov.cn
Tel: 86-10-6855 1118

Ministry of Foreign Affairs
225 Chaoyangmennei Da Jie,
Beijing 100701
Tel: 86-10-6513 5566

**General Administration of
Customs**
6 Jiangguomennei Da Jie,
Beijing 100730
Tel: 86-10-6519 4114

Ministry of Public Security
14 Dongchangan Jie, Beijing
100741
Tel: 86-10-6512 2779

National Statistic Bureau
www.stats.gov.cn
Tel: 86-10-6857 3311

National Tourist
Administration
A9 Jianguomennei Da Jie,
Beijing 100740
Tel: 86-10-6513 8866

People's Bank of China
32 Chengfang Jie, Beijing
100800
Tel: 86-10-6601 5522

State Administration for
Industry & Commerce
8 Sanlihe Donglu, Beijing
100820
Tel: 86-10-6852 2771

State Administration of
Exchange Control
8 Beichen Donglu, Beijing
100101
Tel: 86-10-6491 5738

State Development Planning
Commission
38 Yuetan Nan Jie, Beijing
100045
Tel: 86-10-6850 1240

Gazetted Special Economic Zones

1 **Special Economic Zones
(SEZs)**
  * Hainan
  * Shantou
  * Shenzhen
  * Xiamen
  * Zhuhai

2 **Coastal Development
Cities**
  * Beihai
  * Dalian
  * Fuzhou
  * Guangzhou
  * Lianyungang
  * Nantong
  * Ningbo
  * Qingdao
  * Qinhuangdao
  * Shanghai
  * Tianjin
  * Wenzhou
  * Yantai
  * Zhanjiang

3 **Economic & Technological
Development Zones
(ETDZs)**
  * Beihai
  * Dalian
  * Fuzhou
  * Guangzhou

  * Lianyungang
  * Nantong
  * Ningbo
  * Qingdao
  * Qinhuangdao
  * Shanghai–Caohejing
      Hongqiao
      Minhang
  * Tainjin
  * Wenzhou
  * Yantai
  * Zhanjiang

4 **Coastal Open Economic
Zones (COEZs)**
  * The Guangdong Pearl
    River Delta
  * The South Fujian Min
    River delta
  * The Yangtze River Delta
  * The Laiodong Peninsula
  * The Shandong Peninsula

5 **The High Technological
Zones approved by the
State Council**
  * Changchun
  * Changsha
  * Chengdu
  * Chongqing
  * Fuzhou
  * Guangzhou

* Guilin
* Hangzhou
* Haerbin
* Hefei
* Jinan
* Lanzhou
* Nanjing
* Shenyang
* Shijiazhuang
* Tianjin
* Wuhan
* Xian
* Zhengzhou
* Zhongshan

6 **Five Special High Technological Zones located within the SEZs or ETDZs**
* Dalian–Hi-tech Park
* Hainan–Hi-tech Zone.
* Shanghai–Caohejing
* Shenzhen–Science Park
* Xiamen –Torch Hi-tech Park

Recommended Reading

Kenna, Peggy, *Business China —a practical guide to understanding Chinese business culture*, Lincolnwood, Passport Book, 1994.

Wang Yuan, Zhang Xin Sheng & Rob Goodfellow, *Business Culture in China*, Butterworth-Heinemann Asia , 1998.

Van Kemenade, William, *China, Hong Kong, Taiwan Inc.*, Alfred A. Knopf, New York 1997.

Mackerras, Pradeep Taneja and Young, *China Since 1978*, Addison Wesley Longman, second edition, 1998.

Wilson, Dick, *China The Big Tiger*, Little, Brown & Co., 1996.

Seligman, Scott D., *Chinese Business Etiquette*, Warner Book, 1999.

Murray, Geoffrey, *Doing Business in China—The Last Great Market*, China Library, 1994.

Brahm, Lawrence and Li Daoran, *The Business Guide to China*, Butterworth-Heinemann Asia , 1996.

About the Author

LARRY T L LUAH has accumulated many years of experience working on various projects in China. These include managing the Shanghai JC Mandarin Hotel, and the Lion Group of Companies' Property & Construction Division (China Operation). He was also the founding member and chairman of the Singapore Club (Shanghai).

Index

macro economic policies 18
Mao Zedong 56, 63
market
    local 138
    international 138
meetings 80, 85-90, 97
Memorandum of Understanding
    (MOU) 146, 147
mentality 59
Ministry of Foreign Trade &
    Economic Co-operation
    (MOFTEC) 48, 133, 134,
    146, 148, 156, 157
monetary control 20
Most Favored Nation (MFN) 19

name/business cards 60, 86
National People's Congress
    (NPC) 42, 43, 99, 110
negotiation 79, 85, 88, 97, 140-
    41

official welcomes/send-offs 84
one child policy 64
one-stop services 28
open door policy 13, 27, 48, 100,
    111
opportunities 28, 65, 80, 88, 89

partnerships 33, 138-40, 154
People's Bank of China 99, 100
People's Liberation Army (PLA)
    42
politburo 43
population 15, 21, 23, 63
ports 28, 104, 137, 138, 169, 170
postal services 56

private enterprises (getihu) 35, 36,
    53, 133, 154, 176
productivity 15, 27, 39
protocol 46, 85, 91
public relations 19
Public Security Bureau 111, 157

raw materials 16, 17, 28, 36, 37,
    40, 103, 119, 128, 137
real estate development 81, 154,
    158
religion 60
representative office 23, 32, 67,
    146, 156-58
resources 13, 20, 31, 103, 136,
    137
retail 159, 161
retirees and redundant workers
    142-43
risk 20, 27

safety 177
self interest 144, 165-66
sewerage 51, 53, 54
shopping 176-77
skills 17, 27, 28, 57, 58, 65
social welfare benefits 15, 67, 69
socialist market economy 13
sole proprietorship 33, 146, 154
Special Economic Zone (SEZs)
    28, 66, 122, 126, 127, 183
Standing Committee 42, 43, 110
State Council 42, 43, 99, 104
    108, 111, 116, 120, 152
state enterprises 20, 37, 46
State Planning Commission 152,
    153